Collins 2003

TOWN PLANS OF
BRITAIN

CONTENTS

Tilehurst pangbourne or ? ... Sheatly ←

2003 Edition

Published by Collins
An imprint of HarperCollinsPublishers
77-85 Fulham Palace Road, Hammersmith, London W6 8JB

The HarperCollins website address is: www.**fire**and**water**.com

Copyright © HarperCollinsPublishers Ltd 2002
Mapping © Bartholomew Ltd 1997, 1999, 2000, 2001, 2002

Collins® is a registered trademark of HarperCollinsPublishers Limited

Mapping generated from Bartholomew digital databases

Bartholomew website address is: www.bartholomewmaps.com

Printed in Hong Kong   ISBN 0 00 714102 5   PC11236   MDU

e-mail: roadcheck@harpercollins.co.uk

HarperCollinsPublishers

Johnston · Milford Haven · Neyland · Saunders-foot · Kidwelly (Cydweli) · Burry Port · Pont Abraham S 49
Skomer Island · Pembroke Dock · Pembroke · Tenby · Pembrey · Llanelli 48
Manorbier · Caldey Island · Carmarthen Bay · SWANS
To Rosslare · St Govan's Head · Llanrhidian · S
Worms Head · Mumb
To Cork

Isles of Scilly
Hugh Town · St. Mary's

B r

To Santander (summer only) · To Roscoff

Lundy Island · Ilfracombe A3.99 A4312
Croyde · A361
Barnstaple or Bideford Bay · Braunton · Fremington · Appledore
Hartland Point · Westward Ho! · A39 · Bideford
Hartland · Stibb Cross · Great
Kilkhampton · A388 · A386
Bude · Stratton · A3072 · Highampton
Bude Bay · Holsworthy · A3079 · Okehampt
A39 · A388
Wainhouse Corner · Lydford
Tintagel · Hallworthy · A395 · Launceston · A30 · A386
Delabole · Camelford · Tavistock
St Endellion · Bodmin Moor · A388 · Ho
Padstow · CORNWALL · A390 · Callington · A388
Wadebridge · A389 · St Ive · A386
Trenance · Bodmin · St Columb Major · A38 · Liskeard · A38 · P P
Newquay Cornwall · A30 · A390 · Saltash · Plyr
Newquay · A392 · A3059 · Lostwithiel · Sandplace · Torpoint · Plymstoc
Perranporth · Goonhavern · A3058 · A391 · Par · A387 · East Looe
St Agnes · A390 · St Austell · Polperro
Portreath · Probus · Mevagissey
Redruth · Truro · Tregony
St Ives · Camborne · A39
Zennor · A30 · Penryn · St Mawes
Pendeen · Hayle · A394 · Falmouth
St Just · A3071 · Marazion · A394 · Helston
Penzance · A30 · A394
Land's End · Sennen · Mount's Bay · A3083
Lizard Point · Lizard · St Keverne

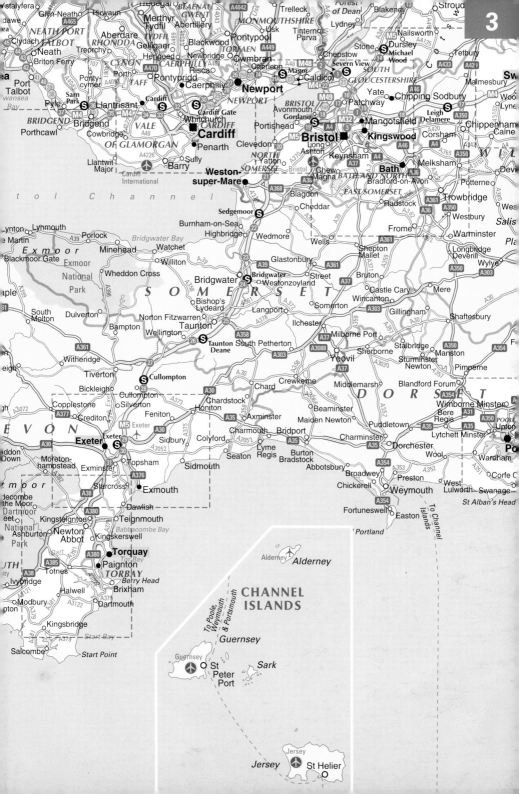

To Dublin

Amlwch

ISLE OF ANGLESEY

To Dublin &
Dun Laoghaire

Moelfre

Anglesey

Llannerch-y-medd

Llandudno
Rhôs-on-Sea

Holyhead

Conwy
Colwyn Bay

Valley

Pentraeth

Llangoed

Conwy Bay

A55

Abergele

Holy
Island

Llangefni

Beaumaris

Llanfairfechan
Llanfair Glan Conwy

Llanfa
Talha

A55

Bangor

A5

Llanfairpwllgwyngyll

Menai Bridge

A470

A548
Llans

Bethesda

A5
CONWY

Caernarfon

A4086

Llanberis

Capel
Curig

Llanrwst

A543

Menai Strait

A4086

Snowdon
(Yr Wyddfa)

Betws-y-coed

Llanwnda

A470

Llandwrog

A487

Snowdonia
1085

A498

A5

Llanllyfni

Beddgelert

A4085

Blaenau
Ffestiniog

Pentrefoela

Llanaelhaearn

A499

Dolbenmaen

A4212

Nefyn

Tremadog

Ffestiniog

Ll *e* *y* *n* *P* *e* *n* *i* *n* *s* *u* *l* *a*

Criccieth

Porthmadog

*Llyn Teg
(Bala La*

Pwllheli

*Tremadog
Bay*

Llyn
Trawsfynydd

Trawsfynydd

Bala

Llanbedrog

Harlech

Llanuwchllyn

Aberdaron

Absersoch

National

A470

A494

GWYNEDD

Bardsey

A496

Llanelltyd

Barmouth

Dolgellau

A470

Mallwyd

A45

A493

Llangelynin

Park

A487

Corris

Llang

Tywyn

Machynlleth

A489

C *a* *r* *d* *i* *g* *a* *n*

Aberdyfi

A470

Eglwys Fach

Dyfi

Llanv

B *a* *y*

Aberystwyth

A44

Llang

A4120

Devil's
Bridge

A487

A495

A470

Llanrhystud

Rhayader

Pontrhydfendigaid
Cross Inn

Aberaeron

CEREDIGION

New Quay

Llanarth

Tregaron

To Rosslare

Aberporth

Synod Inn

A487

Lampeter

Llanwrty
Wells

Cardigan

A484

Llandysul

Llanybydder

Pumsaint

Newport

A475

A482

Goodwick

A487

Newcastle
Emlyn

Llangeler

Llansawel

Llandovery

Fishguard

Crymych

Teifi

A484

A485

A40

**Pembrokeshire Coast
National Park**

Mynydd Preseli

A40

Sennybridge

St David's
Head

PEMBROKESHIRE

Cynwyl
Elfed

Llandeilo

A40

Brec

St David's

A487

A40

Llanegwad

A4069

Nation

*Ramsey
Island*

*St Bride's
Bay*

Llandissilio

Carmarthen

A476

Brynamman

Park

Haverfordwest

A40

Whitland

CARMARTHENSHIRE

A483

802

A407

Broad Haven

A4076

Narberth

St Clears

A48

Tywi

Glyn-Neath

Johnston

Templeton

A477

A40

A4066

Ammanford

A474

A465

Treorchy

Milford Haven

Pont Abraham

Ystalyfera

**NEATH PORT
TALBOT**

*Skomer
Island*

Neyland

Saunders-
foot

Kidwelly
(Cydweli)

M4

Pontardawe

To Rosslare

Pembroke
Dock

Pembroke

Tenby

Burry
Port

Swansea

Clydach
Neath

Pembrey

Llanelli

Morriston

SCALE

0   10   20 miles

0   10   20   30 km

1:1,000,000 16 miles to 1 inch / 10 kilometres to 1 cm

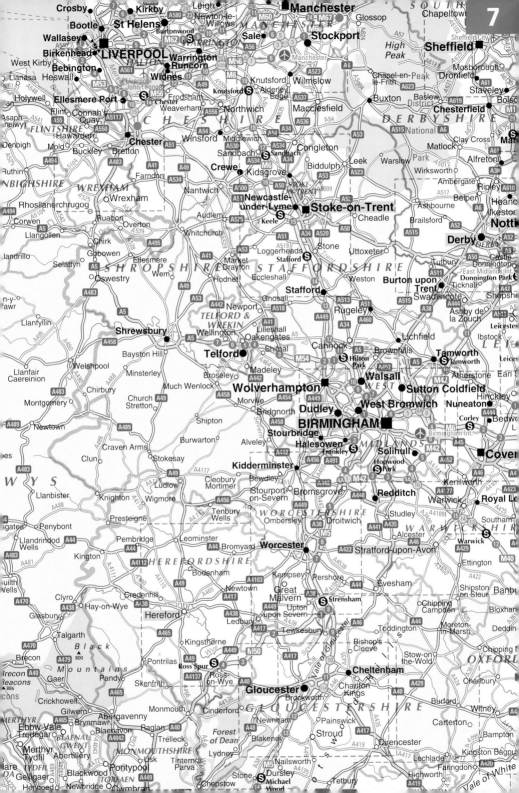

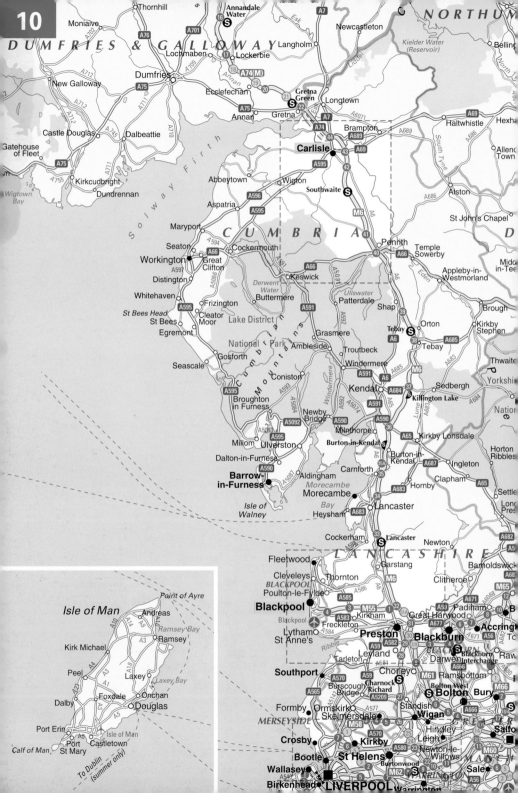

DUMFRIES & GALLOWAY

NORTHUM

Thornhill
Annandale
Water
Moniaive
A7
Newcastleton
Kielder Water
(Reservoir)
Bellin

A701
A76
Langholm
Lochmaben
Lockerbie
Esk
NORTHU

New Galloway
A712
Dumfries
Ecclefechan
A74(M)
Gretna
Green
Longtown
Brampton
A689
A686
Haltwhistle
Hexha

Castle Douglas
Dalbeattie
A711
Annan
Gretna
A7
A6071
Carlisle
A69
A689
South Tyne
Allend
Town

Gatehouse
of Fleet
A75
Solway Firth
Abbeytown
Wigton
Southwaite
A595
A69
A686
Alston
St John's Chapel

Kirkcudbright
Dundrennan
Wigtown
Bay
Maryport
A596
A6
Penrith
Temple
Sowerby
Appleby-in-Westmorland
Mid
in-Tee

Seaton
Workington
A66
Great
Clifton
Cockermouth
A66
Keswick
Derwent
Water
Ullswater
Patterdale
A66
Penrith
A686
Brough
Kirkby
Stephen

Distington
Whitehaven
St Bees Head
St Bees
Cleator
Moor
Frizington
Buttermere
Lake District
Grasmere
Ambleside
Shap
Tebay
A6
Orton
Tebay
A685

Egremont
Gosforth
National Park
Coniston
Troutbeck
Windermere
Kendal
Sedbergh
Thwaite
Yorkshi

Seascale
Broughton
in Furness
Newby
Bridge
Killington Lake
Kirkby Lonsdale
Horton
Ribblesd

Millom
Ulverston
Dalton-in-Furness
Aldingham
Carnforth
Burton-in-Kendal
Ingleton
Clapham
Settle
Long
Pres

Barrow-in-Furness
Morecambe
Bay
Heysham
Morecambe
Lancaster
Hornby

Isle of
Walney
Cockerham
Lancaster
Newton
LANCASHIRE
A682

Fleetwood
Cleveleys
Thornton
Garstang
Barnoldswick
M6
M65

Poulton-le-Fylde
BLACKPOOL
Blackpool
Clitheroe
Padiham
Accring

Lytham
St Anne's
Kirkham
Freckleton
Great Harwood
Blackburn
Raw

Southport
Tarleton
Leyland
Preston
Chorley
Darwen
Blackburn
Interchange

Formby
Burscough
Bridge
Charnock
Richard
Standish
Wigan
Bolton West
Bolton
Bury
M66

Crosby
Ormskirk
Skelmersdale
Hindley
Leigh
Newton-le-Willows
Salfo

Bootle
Kirkby
St Helens
Burtonwood
Sale
Warrington

Wallasey
Birkenhead
LIVERPOOL
M62

Isle of Man

Point of Ayre
Andreas
Ramsey Bay
Ramsey
Kirk Michael
Peel
Laxey
Laxey Bay
Dalby
Foxdale
Onchan
Douglas
Port Erin
Port
St Mary
Calf of Man
Isle of Man
Castletown
To Dublin
(summer only)

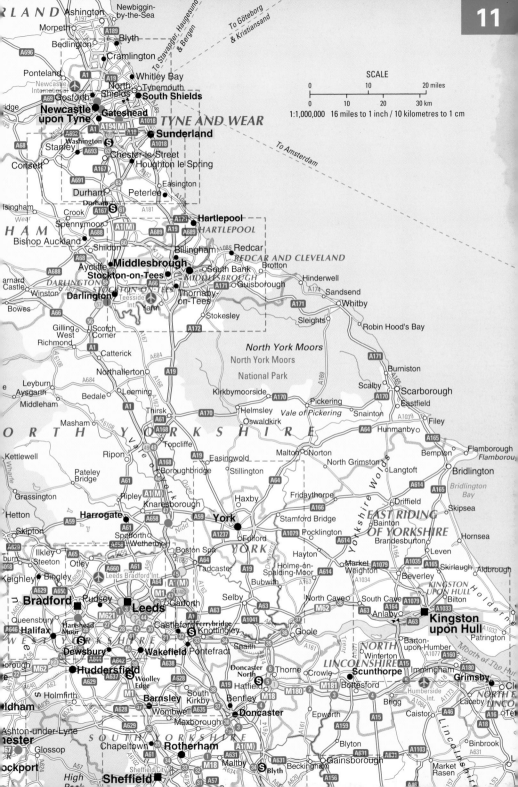

SCALE

0   10   20 miles

0   10   20   30 km

1:1,000,000 16 miles to 1 inch / 10 kilometres to 1 cm

To Kirkwall

To Stromness

To Lerwick

Berriedale

Helmsdale

Tarbat Ness

Portmahomack

Hopeman
Lossiemouth
Portknockie
Cullen
Portsoy
Macduff
Rosehearty
Fraserburgh
Inverallochy

Burghead
Buckie
Banff
Rattray
Head

Findhorn
Elgin
Fochabers
Aberchirder
Strichen
Crimond

Kinloss
Forres
New Pitsligo
Mintlaw

Dava
Rothes
Keith
Bogniebrae
Turriff
New Deer
Peterhead

Craigellachie
Huntly
Boddam

Grantown-on-Spey
Dufftown
Marypark
Strathbogie
Cruden Bay

Dulnain Bridge
MORAY
Insch
Oldmeldrum
Elrick
Newburgh

Carrbridge
Boat of Garten
Mossat
ABERDEENSHIRE
Inverurie
Kintore

Tomintoul
Kemnay
Aberdeen
Dyce

Ben Macdui
Tillyfourie
Westhill
Aberdeen

Mountains
Torphins
Peterculter
ABERDEEN

Braemar
Aboyne
Banchory
Portlethen

Ballater

Stonehaven

North Esk
Fettercairn
Inverbervie

Clova
Laurencekirk

Spittal of Glenshee
Hillside
Brechin
Montrose

Killiecrankie
Tannadice

Kirkmichael
Pitlochry
ANGUS
Kirriemuir
Friockheim

Ballinluig
Forfar
Carmyllie
Arbroath

Strath Tay
Blairgowrie
Glamis
Carnoustie

Dunkeld
Coupar Angus
DUNDEE
Broughty Ferry

ROSS
Methven
New Scone
Dundee
Tayport

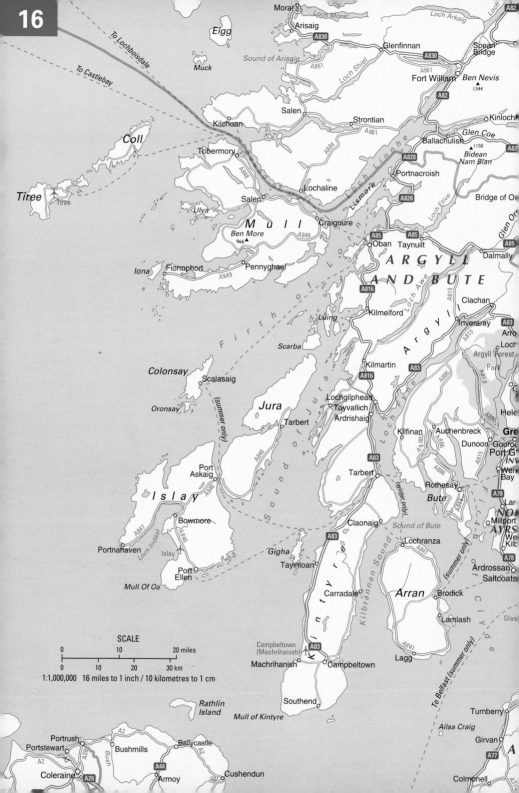

To Lochboisdale
To Castlebay

Eigg
Muck

Morar
Arisaig
A830
Glenfinnan
A830
Spean
Bridge

Sound of Arisaig
A861
Loch Arkaig
A82

Loch Shiel
A861
Fort William
Ben Nevis
1344
A82

Coll
Kilchoan
Salen
Strontian
A861
Kinloch
A82

Tobermory
A848
Glen Coe
Ballachulish
1150
A828

Tiree
Tiree
Lochaline
Portnacroish
Bidean
Nam Bian
A82
Bridge of O

Salen
Craignure
A828
Loch Etive

Mull
Ben More
966
A849
Oban
Taynuilt
A85
Dalmally
A85

Ulva

Iona
Fionnphort
Pennyghael
A849

ARGYLL
AND BUTE

Luing
Kilmelford
Clachan

Scarba
Loch Awe
A816
Inveraray
A83
Arro
Loch

Colonsay
Scalasaig
Argyll Forest
Park

Oronsay

Jura
Kilmartin
A816
A83
Helc

Tarbert
Lochgilphead
Tayvallich
Ardrishaig
Kilfinan
Auchenbreck
Gre
Dunoon
Gouro
Port G
INV

Port
Askaig
A846
A83
Tarbert
Rothesay
Wen
Bay

Islay
A847
Bowmore
Bute
Lar
Millport
We
Kil

Portnahaven
Loch Indaal
A846
Islay
Claonaig
Lochranza
Sound of Bute
A841
A78

Port
Ellen
Gigha
Tayinloan
Ardrossan
Saltcoats
A78

Mull Of Oa
Carradale
Arran
Brodick

SCALE
0   10   20 miles
0 10 20 30 km
1:1,000,000 16 miles to 1 inch / 10 kilometres to 1 cm

Campbeltown
(Machrihanish)
A83
Lamlash

Machrihanish
Campbeltown
Lagg

Southend

Rathlin
Island
Mull of Kintyre
Turnberry

Ailsa Craig
Girvan

Portrush
Portstewart
A2
Bushmills
Ballycastle
A2
Cushendun
A77
A

Coleraine
A26
Armoy
A44
Colmonell

Kintyre
Kilbrannan Sound
Loch Fyne
Firth of Clyde
Firth of Lorn
Sound of Jura
Loch Linnhe
Lismore
Glen Or

Rubha Robhanais

Port Nis

Barabhas

Tolsta Head

Carlabhagh

Loch a' Tuath

Port nan Giúran

Great Bernera

Stornoway (Steornabhagh)

Miavaig

Stornoway

Gearraidh na h-Aibhne

Lewis (Eilean Leodhais)

Loch Langavat

Scarp

Kebock Head

North Harris (Ceann a Tuathna Hearadh)

An Tairbeart

Shiant Islands

Rubha Reidh

WESTERN ISLES (NA H-EILEANAN AN IAR)

Scalpay (Eilean Scalpaigh)

Taobh Tuath

South Harris

Pabbay

Roghadal

Sound of Harris

Rubha Hunish

Kilmaluag

Poolewe

Gairloch

Baile Mhartainn

North Uist (Uibhist a' Tuath)

Lochmaddy (Loch na Madadh)

Uig

Loch Snizort

Rona

Sound of Raas

Shieldaig

Heisker or Monach Islands

Benbecula Aerodrome

719

Little Minch

Loch Dunvegan

A87

A855

The Minch

To Ullapool

Su

Benbecula (Beinn na Faoghla)

Dunvegan

A850

Borve

Portree

Raasay

Inner Sound

Lochcarr

Skye

Bracadale

Loch Bracadale

South Uist (Uibhist a' Deas)

Sligachan

A87

Scalpay

Kyle of Lochalsh

A87

Kyleakin

Cuillin Hills

Broadford

928

Blaven (Bla Bheinn)

Lochboisdale (Loch Baghasdail)

Soay

Elgol

Loch Eishort

Sound of Sleat

Loch Hourn

Eriskay (Eiriosgaigh)

Canna

Ardvasar

Knoydart

Barra (Eilean Barraigh)

Barra

Castlebay (Bagh a' Chaisteil)

Rum (Rhum)

Mallaig

Morar

Loch Nevis

Loch Morar

Vatersay (Bhatarsaigh)

To Oban

Eigg

Arisaig

A830

Sound of Arisaig

Pabaigh (Pabaigh)

A861

Mingulay (Miughalaigh)

To Oban

Muck

Loch Shi

Salen

Tarbert/Loch Tarber

SHETLAND ISLANDS

Herma Ness
Unst
Haroldswick
Baltasound
Belmont
Gutcher
Oddsta
A968
South-haa
Yell
Funzie
A968
Hillswick
Toft
Ulsta
Out Skerries
St. Magnus Bay
Brae
Whalsey
A970
Vidlin
Symbister
Laxo
Sandness
Shetland
Aith
A971
Walls
Bressay
Scalloway
Lerwick
A970
To Bergen, Seydisfjordur & Torshavn (all summer only)
Sumburgh
A970
Sumburgh
Sumburgh Head
To Stromness
To Aberdeen

ORKNEY ISLANDS

North Ronaldsay
Papa Westray
Pierowall
Westray
Sanday
Westray Firth
Rousay
Eday
Egilsay
Stronsay
Tingwall
Shapinsay
A966
A967
Mainland
Orkney
Kirkwall
Stromness
Kirkwall
A964
A961
A960
Gritley
Scapa Flow
Hoy
St. Margaret's Hope
Flotta
South Ronaldsay
Burwick
To Lerwick
To Scrabster
Brough Ness
Pentland Skerries
land Firth
To Aberdeen
Dunnet Head
Island of Stroma
John 'o' Groats
Duncansby Head
Gills Bay
Castletown
A836
A9
Sinclair's Bay
alkirk
Watten
Wick
Mybster
A882
Wick
(summer only)
To Invergordon

Cape Wrath
Strathy Point
Dunnet Head
Island of Stroma
John 'o' Groats
De Ho
Flotta
Pentland Firth
(summer only)
B
Durness
Strathy
Dounreay
Scrabster
Thurso
Castletown
A838
A836
Bettyhill
A836
Thurso
A9
Gills Bay
To Stromness
Rhiconich
Tongue
Ben Hope
927
Strathnaver
Strath Halladale
A897
Halkirk
Sinclair' Bay
Wick
Laxford Bridge
Forsinard
Caithness
Mybster
A882
Watten
Scourie
A894
A838
Strathmore
Loch More
Altnaharra
Kinbrace
A897
Latheron
Wick
A9
Ulbster
Unapool
Sutherland
A836
Thurso
A99
A837
HIGHLAND
Loch Shin
A838
A839
Berriedale
A897
A836
Helmsdale
Helmsdale
chinver
Ledmore
Elphin

Key to approach map symbols

M5 — Motorway (full access)

30 / 29 — Motorway junction (limited access)

Maidstone — Motorway service area with off road / full / limited access (Birch / Sarn)

A48 — Primary route (dual / single)

Primary route with passing places

A30 — 'A' road (dual / single)

'A' road with passing places

B1403 — 'B' road (dual / single)

'B' road with passing places

Minor road

Restricted access due to road condition or private ownership

Road projected or under construction

Multi-level junction

Roundabout

10 — Road distance in miles

Road tunnel

Steep hill (arrows point downhill)

Level crossing / Toll

Car ferry route & journey times; daytime and (night-time)

Railway line and station

Railway tunnel

Airport with scheduled services

Heliport

Park and Ride site

Built up area

Town / Village / Other settlement

National boundary

National / Regional park

Forest park boundary

Danger Zone — Military range

Woodland

468 / 941 — Spot height / Summit height in metres

Beach

Lake / Dam / River / Waterfall

Canal / Dry canal / Canal tunnel

A selection of tourist detail is shown on the mapping. It is advisable to check with the local tourist information office regarding opening times and facilities available.

Tourist information office (all year)

Tourist information office (seasonal)

Ancient monument

1738 — Battlefield

Castle

Country park

Ecclesiastical building

Factory shop village

Garden

Golf course

Historic house (with or without garden)

Major sports venue

Motor racing circuit

Museum / Art gallery

Nature reserve

Preserved railway

Racecourse

Theme park

Wildlife park or Zoo

Other interesting feature

(NT) (NTS) — National Trust / National Trust for Scotland property

Key to town plan symbols

Motorway

Primary route (dual)

'A' road (dual)

'B' road (dual)

Through route (dual)

Restricted access / Pedestrian street

Tourist building

Important building

Higher Education building

Hospital

Cemetery

Recreation area / Open space

P — Car park / Park and Ride site

Railway line / Station

Underground / Metro / Light rail station

Ecclesiastical building

Tourist information centre

One way arrow

STD Code 01224

ABERDEEN

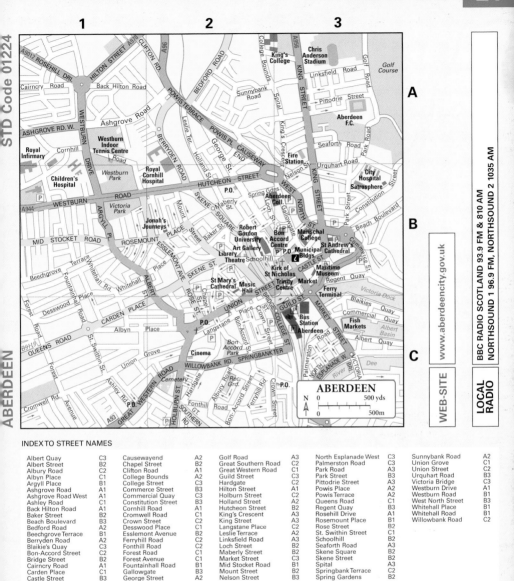

www.aberdeencity.gov.uk — WEB-SITE

BBC RADIO SCOTLAND 93.9 FM & 810 AM
NORTHSOUND 1 96.9 FM, NORTHSOUND 2 1035 AM — LOCAL RADIO

ABERDEEN
N 0   500 yds
   0   500m

INDEX TO STREET NAMES

TOURIST INFORMATION ☎ 01224 632727
ST. NICHOLAS HOUSE, BROAD STREET,
ABERDEEN, AB9 1DE

HOSPITAL A & E ☎ 01224 681818
ABERDEEN ROYAL INFIRMARY, FORESTERHILL,
ABERDEEN, AB25 2ZN

COUNCIL OFFICE ☎ 01224 522000
TOWN HOUSE, BROAD STREET,
ABERDEEN, AB10 1FY

Aberdeen Population: 189,707. City, cathedral and university city and commercial centre on E coast 57m/92km NE of Dundee. Known as 'The Granite City', local stone having been used in many of its buildings. By 13c, Aberdeen had become an important centre for trade and fishing and remains a major port and commercial base. In 19c shipbuilding brought great prosperity to the city. These industries had receded by mid 20c but the city's prospects were transformed when North Sea oil was discovered in 1970, turning it into a city of great wealth. St. Machar's Cathedral at Old Aberdeen. Many museums and art galleries. Extensive flower gardens. Airport at Dyce, 6m/9km NW of Aberdeen.

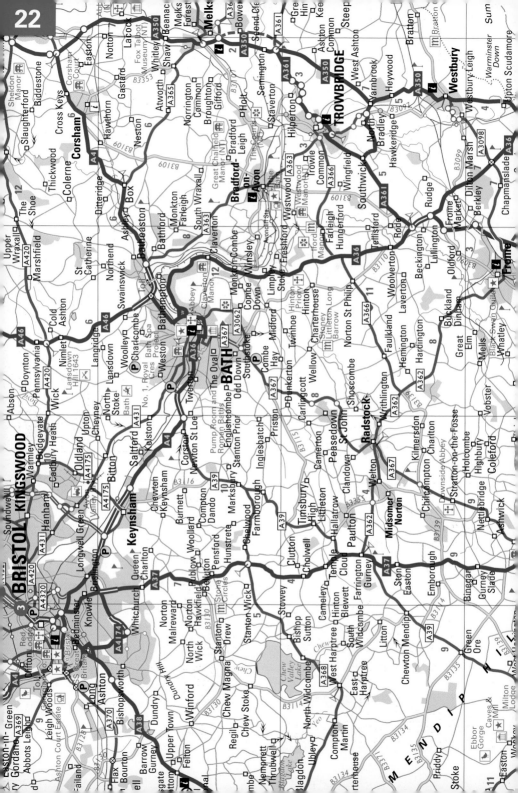

BATH   Bath and N.E. Somerset   STD Code 01225

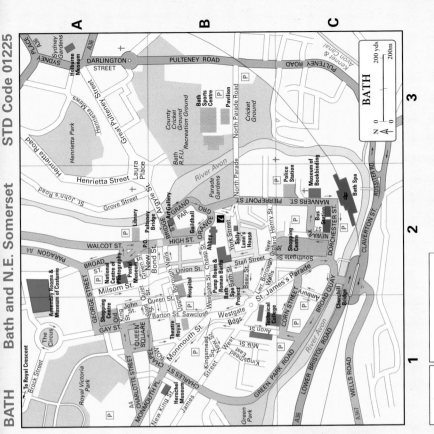

INDEX TO STREET NAMES

Ambury	C1
Argyle Street	B2
Avon Street	B1
Barton Street	B1
Bath Street	B2
Beau Street	B2
Bridge Street	B2
Broad Quay	C1
Broad Street	A2
Brock Street	A1
Chapel Row	B1
Charles Street	A2
Charlotte Street	A1
Cheap Street	B2
Claverton Street	C1
Corn Street	C1
Darlington Street	A3
Dorchester Street	C2
Gay Street	A1
George Street	A1
Grand Parade	B2
Great Pulteney Street	A3
Green Park Road	B1
Green Street	A2
Grove Street	A2
Henrietta Mews	A3
Henrietta Road	A2

Henrietta Street	C1
Henry Street	B2
High Street	B1
James Street West	B1
John Street	B2
Kingsmead East	B2
Laura Place	C1
Lower Borough Walls	A2
Lower Bristol Road	C1
Manvers Street	A1
Milk Street	B1
Milsom Street	A2
Monmouth Place	A1
Monmouth Street	B2
Newark Street	C2
New Bond Street	B1
New King Street	B2
New Orchard Street	B2
New Street	B1
North Parade	B2
North Parade Road	B3
Old King Street	A1
Orange Grove	B2
Paragon	A2
Pierrepont Street	B2
Pulteney Road	B3
Queen Street	B1

Quiet Street	A1
Rossiter Road	C2
St. James's Parade	B1
Sawclose	A2
Southgate Street	B1
Stall Street	C2
Sydney Place	A3
The Circus	A1
Union Street	B2
Upper Borough Walls	B1
Walcot Street	A2
Wells Road	C1
Westgate Buildings	B1
Westgate Street	B2
Wood Street	A1
York Street	B2

TOURIST INFORMATION ☎ 01225 477101
ABBEY CAMBERS, ABBEY CHURCHYARD,
BATH, BA1 1LY

HOSPITAL A & E ☎ 01225 428331
ROYAL UNITED HOSPITAL, COMBE PARK,
BATH, BA1 3NG

COUNCIL OFFICE ☎ 01225 477000
THE GUILDHALL, HIGH STREET,
BATH, BA1 5AW

WEB-SITE   www.bathnes.gov.uk

LOCAL RADIO   BBC RADIO BRISTOL 1548 AM & 104.6 FM
CLASSIC GOLD 1260 AM, 103 GWR FM 103 FM

Bath *B. & N.E.Som.* Population: 85,202. City, spa on River Avon, 11m/18km SE of Bristol. Abbey church rebuilt 1501. Natural hot springs unique in Britain drew Romans to Bath, which they named 'Aquae Sulis'. Roman baths and 18c Pump Room are open to visitors. In 18c, it was most fashionable resort in country. Many Georgian buildings and elegant crescents remain, including The Circus and Royal Crescent. Museum of Costume in restored Assembly Rooms. Holds annual summer music festival. American Museum housed in Claverton Manor and University 3m/4km SE.

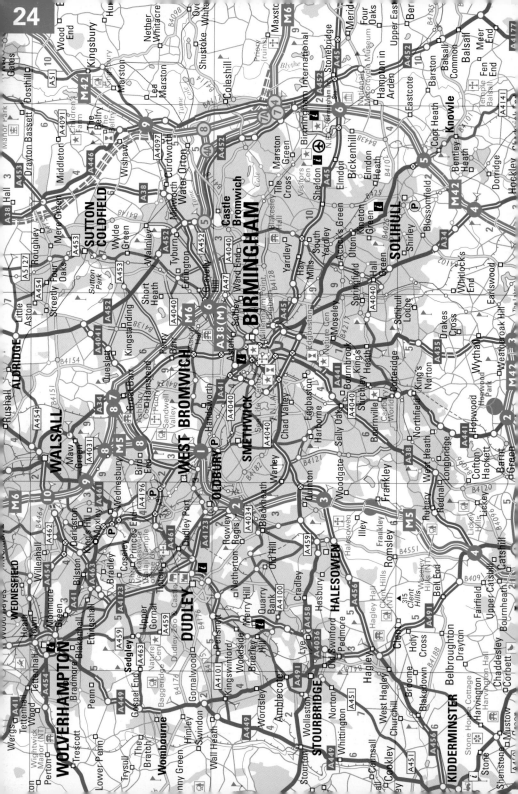

BIRMINGHAM **West Midlands** **STD Code 0121**

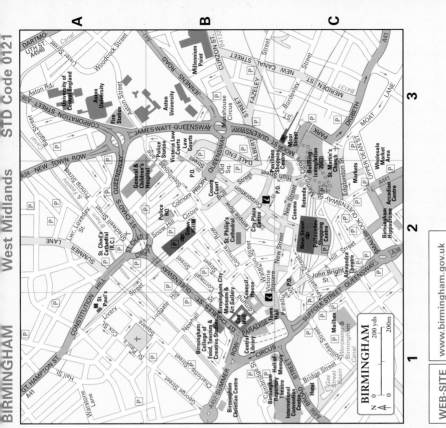

WEB-SITE www.birmingham.gov.uk

LOCAL RADIO
BBC RADIO WM 95.6 FM
RADIO XL 1296 AM, BRMB 96.4 FM, HEART FM 100.7 FM, GALAXY 102.2 FM

INDEX TO STREET NAMES

TOURIST INFORMATION ☎ 0121 643 2514
2 CITY ARCADE, BIRMINGHAM,
WEST MIDLANDS, B2 4TX

HOSPITAL A & E ☎ 0121 554 3801
CITY HOSPITAL, DUDLEY ROAD,
BIRMINGHAM, B18 7QH

COUNCIL OFFICE ☎ 0121 303 9944
COUNCIL HOUSE, VICTORIA SQUARE,
BIRMINGHAM, B1 1BB

Birmingham *W.Mid.* Population: 965,928. City, England's second city and manufacturing, commercial and communications centre, 100m/160km NW of London. Birmingham was home to many pioneers of industrial revolution. Current economic trend is towards post-industrial activities, concentrating on convention and exhibition trades and tourism. To S of city is planned village of Bournville, established by Quaker chocolate magnates George and Richard Cadbury in 1879, influenced by utopian ideas of William Morris. Universities. City has many galleries and museums, particularly around 19c Victoria and Chamberlain Squares. Anglican and Catholic cathedrals. Birmingham International Airport 7m/11km E of city centre.

STD Code 01253

BLACKPOOL

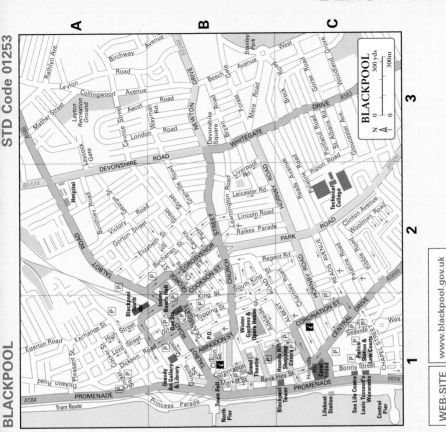

INDEX TO STREET NAMES

Abingdon Street	B1	Devonshire Road	A2
Adelaide Street	B1	Devonshire Square	B3
Albert Road	C1	Dickson Road	A1
Ascot Road	A3	Egerton Road	A1
Bank Hey Street	B1	Elizabeth Street	A2
Beech Avenue West	B3	Exchange Street	A1
Birchway Avenue	A3	Forest Gate	B3
Bonny Street	C1	George Street	B2/A2
Boothley Road	A2	Gloucester Avenue	C3
Breck Road	C3	Gorse Road	A2
Bryan Road	B3	Gorton Street	A2
Buchanan Street	B2	Granville Road	B2
Caunce Street	B2/A3	Grosvenor Street	B2
Central Drive	C1	High Street	A1
Chapel Street	C1	Hornby Road	C1
Charles Street	B2	Hounds Hill	C1
Charnley Road	C1	King Street	B1
Church Street	B2	Laycock Gate	A3
Clifton Street	B1	Layton Road	A3
Clinton Avenue	C2	Leamington Road	B2
Cocker Square	A1	Leicester Road	B2
Cocker Street	A1	Lincoln Road	B2
Collingwood Avenue	A3	Liverpool Road	B2
Cookson Street	B2	London Road	A3
Coronation Street	C1	Lord Street	A1
Corporation Street	B1	Market Street	B1
Deansgate	B1	Mather Street	A3

Mere Road	B3
Newton Drive	B3
Palatine Road	C2
Park Road	C2
Peter Street	B2
Pleasant Street	A1
Portland Road	C3
Princess Parade	B1
Promenade	A1/C1
Queens Square	B1
Queen Street	A2
Rathlyn Avenue	A3
Reads Avenue	C2
Regent Road	B2
Ribble Road	C2
Ripon Road	C3
St. Albans Road	C3
Seaside Way	C1
South King Street	B1/A2
Talbot Road	B1
Topping Street	B1
Victory Road	A2
Wayman Road	B2
Whitegate Drive	A3
Woodland Grove	B3/C3
Woolman Road	C2

TOURIST INFORMATION ☎ 01253 478222
1 CLIFTON STREET,
BLACKPOOL, FY1 1LY

HOSPITAL A & E ☎ 01253 300000
VICTORIA HOSPITAL, WHINNEY HEYS ROAD,
BLACKPOOL, FY3 8NR

COUNCIL OFFICE ☎ 01253 477477
TOWN HALL, TALBOT SQUARE,
BLACKPOOL, FY1 1NA

Blackpool *B'pool* Population: 146,262. Town, large coastal resort and conference centre on Irish Sea, 15m/24km W of Preston. 19c fashionable resort, still very popular today. 7m/11km long 'Golden Mile' of tram route, beach, piers and amusement arcades. Blackpool Pleasure Beach funfair park, 518ft/158m high Tower entertainment complex, annual autumn Illuminations along 5m/8km of Promenade, Zoo, Sea Life Centre, The Sandcastle indoor pool complex and Winter Gardens. Airport 3m/5km S.

WEB-SITE   www.blackpool.gov.uk

LOCAL RADIO   BBC RADIO LANCASHIRE 104.5 FM
MAGIC 999 AM, RADIO WAVE 96.5 FM, ROCK FM 97.4 FM

STD Code 01202

BOURNEMOUTH

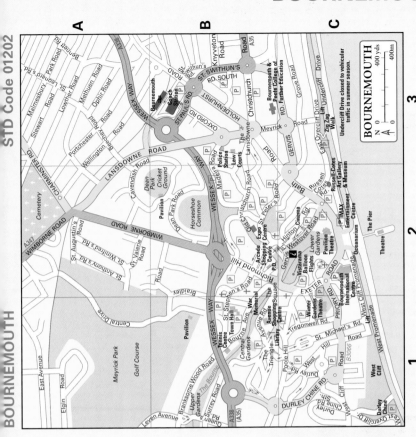

INDEX TO STREET NAMES

Avenue Road	B1	Holdenhurst Road	B3
Bath Road	C2	Knyveton Road	B3
Beechey Road	A3	Lansdowne Road	A2
Bennett Road	A3	Leven Avenue	A1
Bourne Avenue	B1	Lowther Road	A3
Braidley Road	B2	Madeira Road	B2
Branksome Wood Road	B1	Malmesbury Park Road	A3
Cavendish Road	A2	Methuen Road	A3
Central Drive	A1	Meyrick Road	B3
Charminster Road	A2	Old Christchurch Road	B2
Christchurch Road	B3		
Dean Park Road	B2	Ophir Road	A3
Durley Chine Road	C1	Oxford Road	B3
Durley Chine Road South	C1	Poole Hill	C1
		Portchester Road	A2
Durley Road	C1	Priory Road	C1
East Avenue	A1	Queen's Road	B1
East Overcliff Drive	C3	Richmond Hill	B2
Elgin Road	A1	Russell Cotes Road	C2
Exeter Road	C2	St. Anthony's Road	A2
Gervis Place	C2	St. Augustin's Road	A2
Gervis Road	C3	St. Leonard's Road	A2
Grove Road	C3	St. Michael's Road	C1
Hinton Road	C2	St. Pauls Road	B3

St. Peter's Road	B2		
St. Stephen's Road	B1		
St. Swithun's Road	B3		
St. Swithun's Road South	B3		
St. Winifred's Road	A2		
St. Valerie Raod	A2		
Stewart Raod	A3		
Surrey Road	B1		
The Lansdowne	B3		
The Square	B2		
The Triangle	B1		
Tregonwell Road	C1		
Undercliff Drive	C3		
Wellington Road	A2		
Wessex Way	B1/A3		
West Cliff Promenade	C1		
West Cliff Road	C1		
West Hill Road	C1		
West Overcliff Drive	C1		
West Promenade	C1		
Westover Road	C2		
Wimborne Road	B2		

TOURIST INFORMATION ☎ 0906 802 0234
WESTOVER ROAD,
BOURNEMOUTH, BH1 2BU

HOSPITAL A & E ☎ 01202 303626
ROYAL BOURNEMOUTH HOSPITAL,
CASTLE LANE EAST, BOURNEMOUTH, BH7 7DW

COUNCIL OFFICE ☎ 01202 451451
TOWN HALL, BOURNE AVENUE,
BOURNEMOUTH, BH2 6DY

Bournemouth *Bourne.* Population: 155,488. Town, large seaside resort with mild climate, 24m/39km SW of Southampton. Town developed from a few cottages in 1810 to present conurbation. Sandy beach and pier. Extensive parks and gardens including Compton Acres, a display of international garden styles. Russell-Cotes Art Gallery and Museum houses Victorian and oriental collection. University. Conference, business and shopping centre. Bournemouth International Airport, 5m/8km NE of town centre.

WEB-SITE www.bournemouth.gov.uk

LOCAL RADIO BBC RADIO SOLENT FOR DORSET 103.8 FM
CLASSIC GOLD 828 AM, 2CR FM 102.3 FM, FIRE 107.6 FM

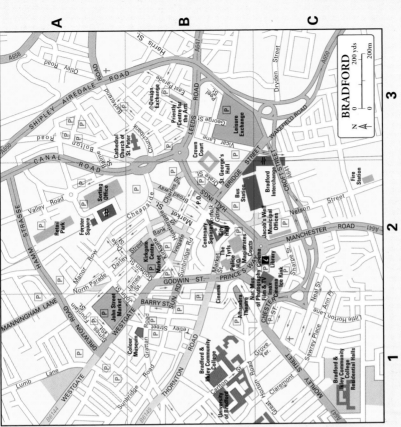

INDEX TO STREET NAMES

Ann Place	C1	George Street	B3
Balme Street	A2	Godwin Street	B2
Bank Street	B2	Grattan Road	B1
Barkerend Road	C1	Great Horton	C1
Barry Street	B1	Road	
Bolton Road	A3	Grove Terrace	C1
Bridge Street	B2	Hall Ings	B2
Broadway	B2	Hamm Strasse	A2
Canal Road	A2	Harris Street	B3
Carlton Street	B1	Hustlergate	B2
Charles Street	B2	Ivegate	B2
Cheapside	B2	James Street	B2
Chester Street	C1	John Street	B1
Churchbank	B3	Kirkgate	B2
Claremont	C1	Leeds Road	B3
Croft Street	C2	Little Horton	C1
Darley Street	A2	Lane	
Drake Street	B2	Lumb Lane	A1
Drewton Road	A1	Manchester	C2
Dryden Street	C3	Road	
Duke Street	A2	Manningham	A1
East Parade	B3	Lane	
Fountain Street	A1	Manor Row	A2
Market Street	B2		
Morley Street	C1		
Neal Street	C1		
Nelson Street	C2		
North Parade	A2		
Otley Road	A3		
Peel Street	B3		
Prince's Way	B2		
Sawrey Place	C1		
Sharpe Street	C2		
Shipley	A3		
Airedale Road	A1		
Simes Street	A1		
Sunbridge Road	B1		
Tetley Street	B1		
Thornton Road	B1		
Valley Road	A2		
Vicar Lane	B3		
Wakefield Road	C3		
Westgate	A1		

TOURIST INFORMATION ☎ 01274 753678
CENTRAL LIBRARY, PRINCES WAY,
BRADFORD, W.YORKS, BD1 1NN

HOSPITAL A & E ☎ 01274 542200
BRADFORD ROYAL INFIRMARY, DUCKWORTH LANE,
BRADFORD, BD9 6RJ

COUNCIL OFFICE ☎ 01274 752111
CITY HALL, CHANNING WAY,
BRADFORD, BD1 1HY

Bradford *W.Yorks.* Population: 289,376. City, industrial city, 8m/13km W of Leeds. Cathedral is former parish church. Previously known as wool capital of the world, Bradford is now less dependent upon the textile industry. Colour Museum documents history of dyeing and textile printing. University. Home to National Museum of Photography, Film and Television with IMAX cinema screen. Model industrial village of Saltaire 3m/5km N planned in 1852 for workers at Salt's Mill which now houses the David Hockney 1853 Gallery. Leeds Bradford International Airport at Yeadon, 6m/10km NE.

WEB-SITE www.bradford.gov.uk

LOCAL RADIO
BBC RADIO LEEDS 102.7 FM
WEST YORKS CLASSIC GOLD 1278 AM, THE PULSE 97.5 FM, SUNRISE RADIO 103.2 FM

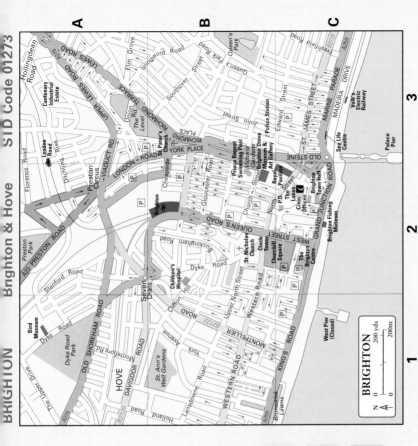

BRIGHTON

0	200 yds
0	200m

INDEX TO STREET NAMES

Buckingham Road	B2	John Street	B3	Richmond Terrace	B3
Cheapside	B2	King's Road	C1	St. James's Street	C3
Church Street	B2	Lansdowne Road	B1	Southover Street	B3
Churchill Square	C2	Lewes Road	A3	Stanford Road	A2
Clifton Hill	B1	London Road	A2	The Lanes	C2
Davigdor Road	A1	Madeira Drive	C3	The Upper Drive	A1
Ditchling Rise	A2	Marine Parade	C3	Union Road	A3
Dyke Road	B2	Montefiore Road	A1	Upper Lewes Road	A3
Edward Street	C3	Montpelier Road	B1	Upper North Street	B2
Elm Grove	A3	North Street	B2	Viaduct Road	A2
Florence Road	A2	Old Shoreham Road	A1	West Street	C2
Freshfield Road	C3	Old Steine	B2	Western Road	B1
Gloucester Road	B2	Preston Circus	C2	York Avenue	B1
Grand Junction Road	A2	Preston Park	B3	York Place	B3
Holland Road	B1	Queen's Park Road	B2	
Hollingdean Road	A3	Queen's Road	A3	
Islingword Road	A3	Richmond Place		

TOURIST INFORMATION ☎ 0906 711 2255
10 BARTHOLOMEW SQUARE,
BRIGHTON, BN1 1JS

HOSPITAL A & E ☎ 01273 696955
ROYAL SUSSEX COUNTY HOSPITAL, EASTERN ROAD,
BRIGHTON, BN2 5BE

COUNCIL OFFICE ☎ 01273 290000
TOWN HALL, BARTHOLOMEWS,
BRIGHTON, BN1 1JA

Brighton *B. & H.* Population: 124,851. Town, seaside resort, sailing and conference centre, 48m/77km S of London. Previously a fishing village known as Brighthelmstone, centred on current Lanes area. Brighton became fashionable as a sea-bathing resort in the 18c. Patronized by the Prince Regent in 1780s who built the Royal Pavilion in Oriental style as a summer palace. Regency squares at Kemp Town. Amusement arcades on 1899 Palace Pier. Annual festivals. Language schools. Universities.

WEB-SITE www.brighton-hove.gov.uk

LOCAL RADIO BBC SOUTHERN COUNTIES RADIO 95.3 FM
CAPITAL GOLD 1323 AM, SOUTHERN FM 103.5

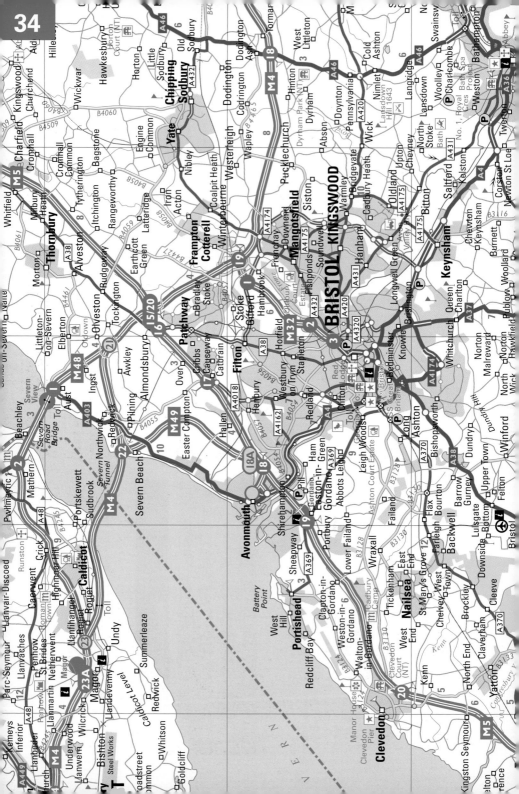

BRISTOL

STD Code 0117

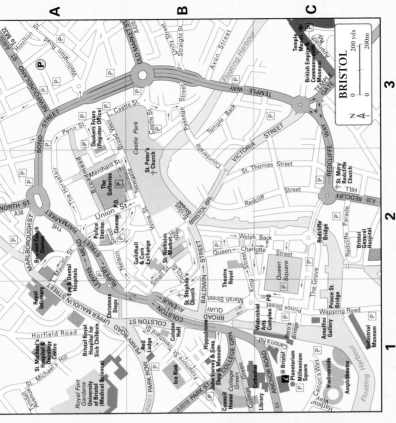

Map labels: A1, A2, A3 / B1, B2, B3 / C1, C2, C3

Key streets and landmarks: Houlton St, Wellington Road, Bond Street, Old Market St, Straight Street, Unity Street, Temple Back, Floating Harbour, Temple Way, Temple Meads, Temple Gate, British Empire & Commonwealth Museum, Penn St, Castle St, Castle Park, Broad Weir, Passage Street, Avon Street, Victoria Street, St. Thomas Street, Redcliff Street, Quakers Friars (Register Office), Broadmead, Merchant St, St. Peter's Church, The Galleries, Newgate, Counterslip, Redcliff Street, St. Mary Redcliffe Church, Redcliffe Hill, North St, Union St, Police Station, Cinema, St. Nicholas Market, High Street, Bristol Bridge, Wine St, Redcliffe Parade, Bus and Coach Station, THE HAYMARKET, Fire & Dental Hospitals, Guildhall & Corn Exchange, St. Stephen's Church, Welsh Back, Queen Charlotte Street, Redcliffe Bridge, Bristol General Hospital, Royal Infirmary, LEWINS MEAD, UPPER MAUDLIN STREET, Christmas Steps, Nelson St, Small St, Baldwin Street, Theatre Royal, King Street, Queen Square, The Grove, Prince St, Prince St Bridge, Wapping Road, St. Michael's Hospital & Oncology Centre, Bristol Royal Hospital for Sick Children, University of Bristol (Medical Science), Horfield Road, COLSTON ST, Colston Hall, Trenchard St, Red Lodge, Hippodrome, John Harvey & Sons Shop & Museum, Watershed Arts Complex, Arnolfini Gallery, Industrial Museum, Royal Fort Gardens, PARK ROW, Frogmore St, Park St, PARK STREET, Ice Rink, Council House, College Green, Cathedral, Library, Canon's Rd, @ Bristol, Planetarium, Millennium Square, Amphitheatre, Harbourside, Harbour Way, Canon's Way, Floating Harbour, A4, A38, A420, A4044, A4018, B4051, B4466

TOURIST INFORMATION ☎ 0117 926 0767
THE ANNEXE, WILDSCREEN WALK, HARBOURSIDE,
BRISTOL, BS1 5UD

HOSPITAL A & E ☎ 0117 923 0000
BRISTOL ROYAL INFIRMARY,
MARLBOROUGH STREET, BRISTOL, BS2 8HW

COUNCIL OFFICE ☎ 0117 922 2000
THE COUNCIL HOUSE, COLLEGE GREEN,
BRISTOL, BS1 5TR

Bristol Population: 407,992. City, 106m/171km W of London. Port on River Avon dates from medieval times. Bristol grew from transatlantic trade in rum, tobacco and slaves. In Georgian times, Bristol's population was second only to London and many Georgian buildings still stand, including the Theatre Royal, the oldest working theatre in the country. Bristol is now a commercial and industrial centre. Cathedral dates from 12c and was originally an abbey. 15c Temple Church tower and walls (English Heritage). Restored iron ship SS Great Britain and Industrial Museum in city docks area. Universities. 245ft/75m high Clifton Suspension Bridge completed in 1864 across the Avon Gorge NW of the city. Bristol International Airport at Lulsgate 7m/11km SW.

WEB-SITE   www.bristol-city.gov.uk

LOCAL RADIO
BBC RADIO BRISTOL 94.9 FM
BRUNEL CLASSIC GOLD 1260 AM, GWR FM 96.3 FM, GALAXY 101 972 FM, STAR 107.3 FM

CAMBRIDGE
Cambridge
Godmanchester
Hemingford Grey
Island Hall
Wood Green Animal Shelter
Fenstanton
Fen Drayton
Over
Swavesey
Rampton
Cottenham
Chittering
Fen
Upware
Wicken
Little Fen
Denny Abbey
River Bank
Adventurers' Fen
Reach
Burwell
Exning
Newmarket Heath
Newmarket
Offord Cluny
Offord D'Arcy
Great Ouse
Hilton
Conington
Boxworth End
Roman Road
Longstanton
Westwick
Waterbeach
Landbeach
Swaffham Prior
Commercial End
Swaffham Bulbeck
Lode
Anglesey Abbey (NT)
Bottisham
Stow cum Quy
Horningsea
Milton
Impington
Histon
Oakington
Girton
Great Paxton
Graveley
Papworth St Agnes
Papworth Everard
Elsworth
Boxworth
Lolworth
Bar Hill
Dry Drayton
Knapwell
Toseland
Yelling
Paxton
Neots
Croxton
Eltisley
Caxton Gibbet
Cambourne
Caxton
Highfields
Hardwick
Madingley
Cambridge American Cemetery & Memorial
Coton
King's Coll Chapel
Univ Botanic Gardens
Chesterton
Fen Ditton
Teversham
Little Wilbraham
Great Wilbraham
Church End
Six Mile Bottom
Dullingham
Westley Waterless
Fulbourn
Cherry Hinton
Gog Magog Hills
Wandlebury
Lark Hall
Brinkley
Weston Colville
West Wratting
Abbotsley
Great Gransden
Little Gransden
Waresley
Bourn
Caldecote
Toft
Kingston
Comberton
Barton
Grantchester
Trumpington
Longstowe
Great Eversden
Little Eversden
Ermine Street
Tetworth
Gamlingay
Hatley St George
East Hatley
Everton
Potton
Cockayne Hatley
Wimpole Hall (NT)
Arrington
Croydon
Wimpole
Orwell
Harlton
Frog End
Haslingfield
Hauxton
Great Shelford
Stapleford
Little Shelford
Harston
Barrington
Newton
Foxton
Shepreth
Wimpole Home Farm (NT)
Docwra's Manor
Granta
Cam
Babraham
Sawston
Duxford Chapel
Whittlesford
Pampisford
Great Abington
Little Abington
Worsted Lodge
Balsham
West Wickham
Hildersham
Linton
Horseheath
Bartlow
Shudy Camps
Linton Zoo & Gdns
Hadstock
Wrestlingworth
Sutton
Tadlow
Cam or Rhee
Wendy
Shingay
Abington Pigotts
Eyeworth
Guilden Morden
Dunton
Biggleswade
Whaddon
Whaddon Gap
Meldreth
Kneesworth
Melbourn
Bassingbourn
Litlington
Steeple
Flint Cross
Bridgefoot
Thriplow
Fowlmere
Duxford
Imperial War Museum
Hinxton
Ickleton
Chrishall Grange
Stump Cross
Great Chesterford
Little Chesterford
Ashdon
Camps End
A14
A11
A10
A505
A1198
A1303
A1304
A1307
A1301
A1134
A428
A603
A1096
A6001
M11
B1046
B1040
B1042
B1368
B1052
B1102
B1103
B1049

CAMBRIDGE   Cambridgeshire   STD Code 01223

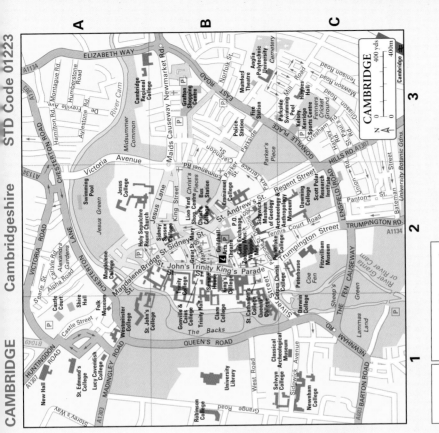

CAMBRIDGE

0   400 yds
0   400m

INDEX TO STREET NAMES

Alpha Road	A2	Humberstone	
Aylestone Road	A3	Road	A3
Barton Road	C1	Huntingdon Road	A2
Bateman Street	C2	Jesus Lane	B2
Carlyle Road	A2	King's Parade	B2
Castle Street	A1	King Street	B2
Chesterton Lane	A2	Lensfield Road	C2
Chesterton Road	A2	Madingley Road	A1
Clarendon Street	B3	Magdalene Bridge	A2
De Freville Avenue	A3	Street	
Downing Street	B2	Maids Causeway	B3
East Road	B3	Market Street	B2
Elizabeth Way	A3	Mawson Road	C3
Emmanuel Road	B2	Mill Road	C3
Fen Causeway, The	C1	Montague Road	A3
Glisson Road	C3	Newmarket Road	B3
Gonville Place	C2	Newnham Road	C1
Grange Road	B1	Norfolk Street	B3
Gresham Road	C3	Panton Street	C2
Hamilton Road	A3	Parker Street	B2
Harvey Road	C3	Parkside	B3
Hills Road	C3	Park Terrace	B2

Pembroke Street	B2		
Queen's Road	B1		
Regent Street	B2		
St. Andrew's			
Street	B2		
St. John's Street	B2		
St. Paul's Road	C3		
Searce Street	A1		
Sidgwick Avenue	C1		
Sidney Street	B2		
Silver Street	C1		
Storey's Way	A1		
Tenison Road	C3		
Tennis Court Road	B2		
Trinity Street	B2		
Trumpington Road	C2		
Trumpington	C1		
Street			
Union Road	C2		
Victoria Avenue	A2		
Victoria Road	A2		
West Road	B1		

TOURIST INFORMATION ☎ 01223 322640
WHEELER STREET, CAMBRIDGE,
CAMBRIDGESHIRE, CB2 3QB

HOSPITAL A & E ☎ 01223 245151
ADDENBROOKE'S HOSPITAL, HILLS ROAD,
CAMBRIDGE, CB2 2QQ

COUNCIL OFFICE ☎ 01223 457000
THE GUILDHALL, MARKET SQUARE,
CAMBRIDGE, CB2 3QJ

Cambridge *Cambs.* Population: 95,682. City, university city on River Cam 49m/79km N of London. First college founded here in 1271. Historic tensions existed between students and townspeople since 14c, and came to a head during Peasants' Revolt of 1381 in which five townsfolk were hanged. Oliver Cromwell was a graduate of Sidney Sussex College and local MP at a time when the University was chiefly Royalist. 1870's saw foundation of first women's colleges, but women were not awarded degrees until after 1947. University's notable graduates include prime ministers, foreign heads of state, literary giants, philosophers and spies. Cambridge boasts many fine museums, art galleries and buildings of interest, including King's College Chapel and Fitzwilliam Museum. Airport at Teversham 3m/4km E.

WEB-SITE   www.cambridge.gov.uk

LOCAL RADIO   BBC RADIO CAMBRIDGESHIRE 96 FM
Q 103 FM, STAR 107.9 FM

MARGATE

HERNE BAY

WHITSTABLE

CANTERBURY

Faversham

Sandwich

Westgate on Sea

Birchington

Acol

Minster

Monkton

Manston

RAF Manston
Spitfire &
Hurricane
Memorial Bldg

Quex House
& Gdns

Tudor House

St Augustine's Cross

Pegwell Bay

Sandwich Flats

Stonar Cut

Great Stonar

Salutation Gdn

Worth

Ham

Hacklinge

Sholden

Northbourne

Betteshanger

Great Mongeham

Ripple

Sutton

Marley Mill Sta

West Studdal

East Studdal

Ashley

West Langdon

East Langdon

Guston

Whitfield

Coldred

Shepherdswell
(Sibertswold)

Woollage Green

Denton

Wootton

Selstead

Lydden

Eythorne

Elvington

Barfrestone

Eastry

Knowlton

Goodnestone

Nonington

Easole Street

Chillenden

Womenswold

Barham

Kingston

Bishopsbourne

Derringstone

Bladbean

Wingmore

Breach

Bossingham

Stelling Minnis

Petham

Waltham

Bodsham Green

Hastingleigh

Lyminge

Lyminge Forest

Elham

Sole Street

Hassell Street

Stone Street

B2068

Sixmile Cottages

Richborough Castle

Roman Amphitheatre

Ash

Weddington

Staple

Wingham

Marshborough

Woodnesborough

Ickham

Wickhambreaux

Stodmarsh

Bramling

Bekesbourne

Patrixbourne

Adisham

Aylesham

Goodnestone Park

Roman Road

Littlebourne

Howletts Wild Animal Park

St Augustine's Abbey

Thanington

Harbledown

Nackington

Lower Hardres

Upper Hardres Court

Street End

Bridge

Chartham

Chartham Hatch

Shalmsford Street

Old Wives Lees

Chilham

Chilham Castle

Shottenden

Molash

Godmersham

Boughton Aluph

Eastwell Park

Charing

Westwell

Westwell Leacon

Challock

Chartham

Crundale

Wye

Brook

Kennington

Waltham

A252

A251

A28

A20

M20

M2

Isle of Thanet

Isle of Harty

ISLE OF SHEPPEY

Eastchurch

Leysdown-on-Sea

Warden

Shell Ness

Seasalter

Swalecliffe

Chestfield

Clapham Hill

Yorkletts

Dargate

Hernhill

Goodnestone

Preston

Oare

Luddenham Court

Uplees

Teynham Sta

Lynsted

Frith

Eastling

Stalisfield Green

Throwley

Whitehill

Ospringe

Maison Dieu

Brogdale Horticultural Trust

North Street

Sheldwich

Badlesmere

Leaveland

Selling

Overland

Boughton Street

Dunkirk

Boughton Lees

Boughton

Sandway

Chilham

Bilting

Beltinge

Reculver

Towers & Reculver Fort

Hillborough

Bishopstone

Broomfield

Hunters Forstal

Herne Common

Maypole

Hoath

Upstreet

Chislet

Marshside

West Stourmouth

East Stourmouth

Grove

Preston

Stodmarsh

Hersden

Westbere

Sturry

Fordwich

Hales Place

Rough Common

Blean

Tyler Hill

Honey Hill

Pean Hill

Broad Oak

Calcott

Wealden Woodlands

Herne

West End

Swalecliffe

Gore Street

Sarre

St Nicholas at Wade

Boyden Gate

Highstead

Chitty

Sarre Penn

Great Stour

Little Stour

Stour

Roman Road

Ware

Cop Street

Westmarsh

Hoaden

Elmstone

Brook

Wingham Well

Twitham

Staple

Knell

Summerfield

Each End

Durlock

Coombe

Roman Road

A2

A28

A257

A256

A258

A2050

A291

A290

A299

A2990

A2033

A28

B2205

B2231

M2

M20

A20

A252

A251

A262

A299

STD Code 01227   **Kent**

CANTERBURY

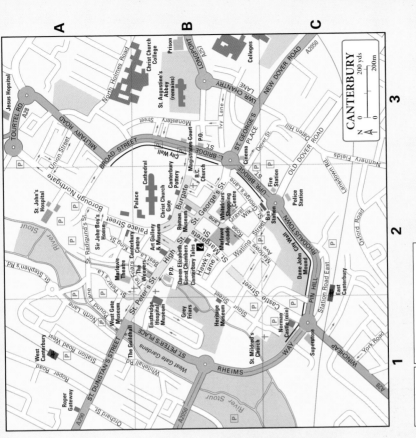

CANTERBURY

0   200 yds
0   200m

N

1   2   3

A   B   C

INDEX TO STREET NAMES

Best Lane	B2
Borough Northgate	A2
Broad Street	A3
Burgate	B2
Castle Street	C1
Dover Street	B3
Gravel Walk	B2
Hawk's Lane	B2
High Street	B2
Ivy Lane	C1
King Street	A1
Lansdown Road	A2
Longport	C2
Lower Bridge Street	B3
Lower Chantry Lane	C2
Marlowe Avenue	C2
Military Road	A3
Monastery Street	B3
New Dover Road	C3
North Holmes Road	A3
North Lane	A1
Nunnery Fields	C3
Oaten Hill	C3
Old Dover Road	C2
Orchard Street	A1
Oxford Road	C2
Palace Street	B2
Pin Hill	C1
Pound Lane	A1
Rheims Way	B1
Rhodaus Town	C2
Roper Road	A1
Rose Lane	B2
St. Dunstan's Street	A1
St. George's Lane	B3
St. George's Place	C2
St. George's Street	B2
St. Margarets Street	B2
St. Peter's Lane	A2
St. Peter's Place	B1
St. Peter's Street	A1
St. Radigund's Street	A2
St. Stephen's Road	A1
Station Road East	C1
Station Road West	A1
Stour Street	B1
The Friar's	B2
Tourtel Road	A3
Union Street	A1
Upper Bridge Street	C2
Watling Street	B2
Whitehall Road	B1
Wincheap	C1
York Road	C1

TOURIST INFORMATION ☎ 01227 766567
34 ST. MARGARET'S STREET,
CANTERBURY, KENT, CT1 2TG

HOSPITAL A & E ☎ 01227 766877
KENT & CANTERBURY HOSPITAL, ETHELBERT ROAD,
CANTERBURY, CT1 3NG

COUNCIL OFFICE ☎ 01227 862000
COUNCIL OFFICES, MILITARY ROAD,
CANTERBURY, CT1 1YW

WEB-SITE   www.canterbury.gov.uk

LOCAL RADIO   BBC RADIO KENT 97.6 FM
INVICTA FM 103.1 FM, 106 CTFM 106 FM

Canterbury *Kent* Population: 36,464. City, premier cathedral city and seat of Primate of Church of England on Great Stour River, 54m/88km E of London. Site of Roman settlement Durovernum. After Romans left, Saxons renamed town Cantwarabyrig. First cathedral in England built on site of current Christ Church Cathedral in AD 602. Thomas à Becket assassinated in Canterbury in 1170, turning Cathedral into great Christian shrine and destination of many pilgrimages, such as those detailed in Geoffrey Chaucer's Canterbury Tales. Becket's tomb destroyed on orders of Henry VIII. Cathedral was backdrop for premiere of T.S. Eliot's play 'Murder in the Cathedral' in 1935. City suffered extensive damage during World War II. Many museums and galleries explaining city's rich heritage. Roman and medieval remains, including city walls. Modern shopping centre; industrial development on outskirts. University of Kent on hill to N.

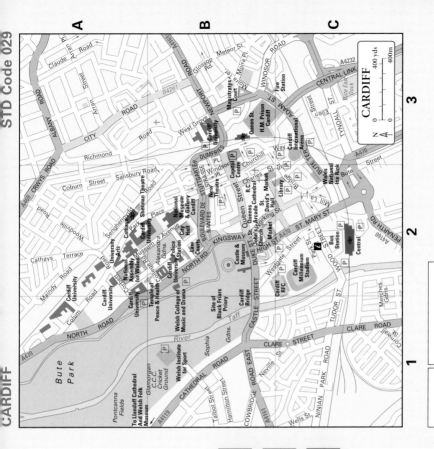

TOURIST INFORMATION ☎ 029 2022 7281
CARDIFF VISITOR CENTRE, 16 WOOD STREET,
CARDIFF, CF10 1ES

HOSPITAL A & E ☎ ☎ 029 2074 7747
CARDIFF UNIVERSITY OF WALES HOSPITAL, HEATH PARK,
CARDIFF, CF14 4XW

COUNCIL OFFICE ☎ 029 2087 2087
THE HELP CENTRE, MARLAND HOUSE, CENTRAL SQUARE,
CARDIFF, CF10 1EP

Cardiff (Caerdydd). Population: 272,129. City, capital of Wales since 1955. Romans founded military fort and small settlement on site of present day Cardiff. Uninhabited between departure of Romans and Norman conquest centuries later. Fishing village until development of coal mining in 19c. Population rose from 1000 in 1801 to 170,000 a century later, with city becoming one of busiest ports in the world. Dock trade collapsed in 1930's. Since establishment as Welsh capital, many governmental, administrative and media organisations have moved to city. Major refurbishment and development programme still under way. Cardiff Bay area now major tourist centre and includes Techniquest, a science discovery centre, and has been selected as the location of the new Welsh Assembly building. Millennium Stadium Cardiff Arms Park is the home of the Welsh Rugby Union and also hosts other sporting and entertainment events. Many museums including National Museum of Wales. Universities.

WEB-SITE www.cardiff.gov.uk

LOCAL RADIO BBC RADIO WALES 96.8 FM
CAPITAL GOLD 1305 & 1359 AM, RED DRAGON FM 103.2 FM

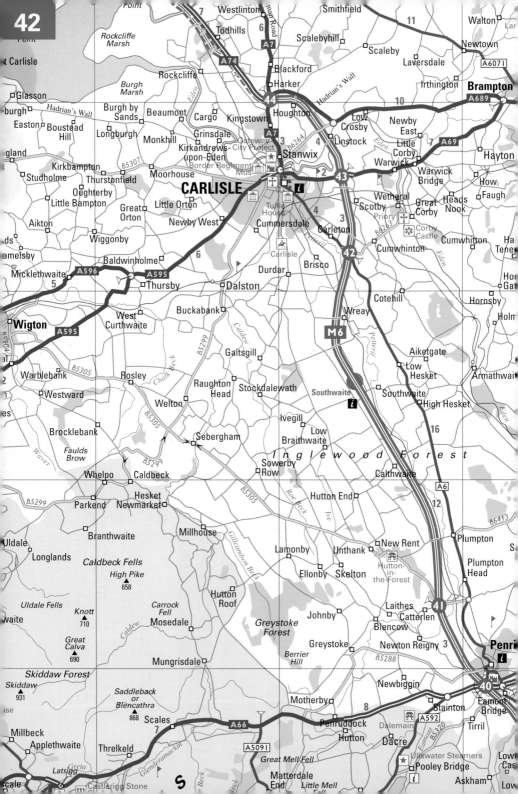

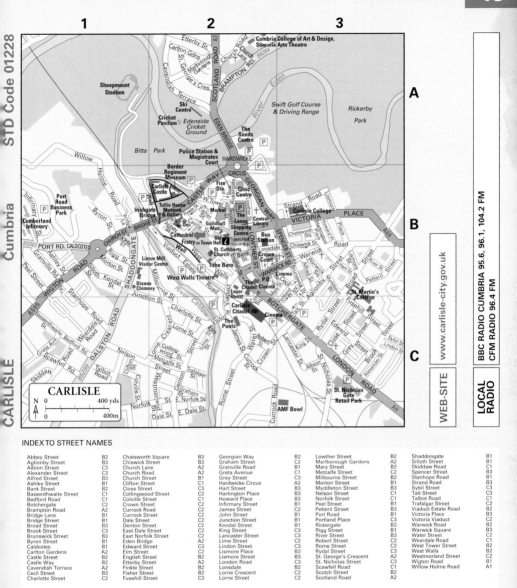

CARLISLE

N 0 — 400 yds
0 — 400m

TOURIST INFORMATION ☎ 01228 625600
OLD TOWN HALL, GREEN MARKET,
CARLISLE, CA3 8JH

HOSPITAL A & E ☎ 01228 523444
CUMBERLAND INFIRMARY, NEWTOWN ROAD,
CARLISLE, CA2 7HY

COUNCIL OFFICE ☎ 01228 817000
CARLISLE CITY COUNCIL, THE CIVIC CENTRE,
CARLISLE, CA3 8QG

Carlisle *Cumb.* Population: 72,439. Cathedral city at confluence of River Eden and River Caldew, 54m/87km W of Newcastle upon Tyne. Once a Roman military base and later fought over by Scots and English, line of Hadrian's wall runs through the northern suburbs. Castle above the River Eden, completed in 12c, houses a military museum. Cathedral partially destroyed by fire in 17c has two surviving bays of 12c and a magnificent East window. Tullie House Museum imaginatively tells of the city's turbulent past. University of Northumbria. Racecourse 2m/4km S. Airport 6m/9km NE.

Left margin:
STD Code 01228
Cumbria
CARLISLE

Right margin:
www.carlisle-city.gov.uk
WEB SITE
BBC RADIO CUMBRIA 95.6, 96.1, 104.2 FM
CFM RADIO 96.4 FM
LOCAL RADIO

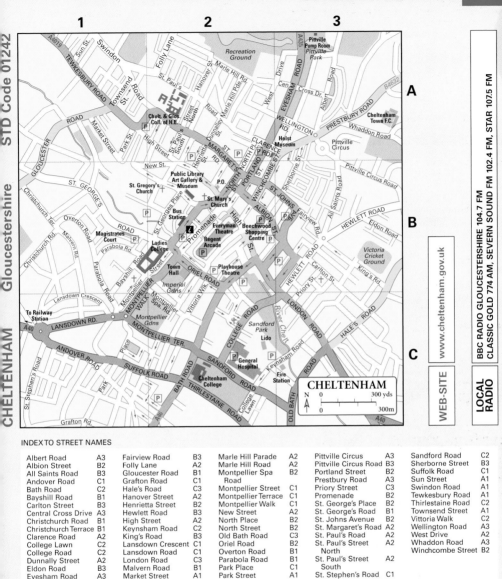

CHELTENHAM Gloucestershire STD Code 01242

CHELTENHAM
N 0 .... 300 yds
0 .... 300m

WEB-SITE www.cheltenham.gov.uk

LOCAL RADIO BBC RADIO GLOUCESTERSHIRE 104.7 FM, CLASSIC GOLD 774 AM, SEVERN SOUND FM 102.4 FM, STAR 107.5 FM

INDEX TO STREET NAMES

Albert Road	A3	Fairview Road	B3	Marle Hill Parade	A2	Pittville Circus	A3	Sandford Road	C2
Albion Street	B2	Folly Lane	A2	Marle Hill Road	A2	Pittville Circus Road	B3	Sherborne Street	B3
All Saints Road	B3	Gloucester Road	B1	Montpellier Spa	B2	Portland Street	B2	Suffolk Road	C1
Andover Road	C1	Grafton Road	C1	Road		Prestbury Road	A3	Sun Street	A1
Bath Road	C2	Hale's Road	C3	Montpellier Street	C1	Priory Street	C3	Swindon Road	A1
Bayshill Road	B1	Hanover Street	A2	Montpellier Terrace	C1	Promenade	B2	Tewkesbury Road	A1
Carlton Street	B3	Henrietta Street	B2	Montpellier Walk	C1	St. George's Place	B2	Thirlestaine Road	C2
Central Cross Drive	A3	Hewlett Road	B3	New Street	A2	St. George's Road	B1	Townsend Street	A1
Christchurch Road	B1	High Street	A2	North Place	B2	St. Johns Avenue	B2	Vittoria Walk	C2
Christchurch Terrace	B1	Keynsham Road	C2	North Street	B2	St. Margaret's Road	A2	Wellington Road	A3
Clarence Road	A2	King's Road	B3	Old Bath Road	C3	St. Paul's Road	A2	West Drive	A2
College Lawn	C2	Lansdown Crescent	C1	Oriel Road	B2	St. Paul's Street	A2	Whaddon Road	A3
College Road	C2	Lansdown Road	C1	Overton Road	B1	North		Winchcombe Street	B2
Dunnally Street	A2	London Road	C3	Parabola Road	B1	St. Paul's Street	A2		
Eldon Road	B3	Malvern Road	B1	Park Place	C1	South			
Evesham Road	A3	Market Street	A1	Park Street	A1	St. Stephen's Road	C1		

TOURIST INFORMATION ☎ 01242 522878
77 THE PROMENADE, CHELTENHAM,
GLOUCESTERSHIRE, GL50 1PP

HOSPITAL A & E ☎ 01242 222222
CHELTENHAM GENERAL HOSPITAL,
SANDFORD ROAD, CHELTENHAM, GL53 7AN

COUNCIL OFFICE ☎ 01242 262626
MUNICIPAL OFFICES, THE PROMENADE,
CHELTENHAM, GL50 1PP

Cheltenham *Glos.* Population: 91,301. Town, largest town in The Cotswolds, 8m/12km NE of Gloucester. Shopping and tourist centre, with some light industry. Mainly residential, with many Regency and Victorian buildings and public gardens. Formerly a spa town, Pittville Pump Room built between 1825 and 1830 overlooks Pittville Park and is now used for concerts. Art Gallery and Museum. Ladies' College founded 1853. Racecourse to the N hosts Cheltenham Gold Cup race meeting, Cheltenham International Music Festival and Festival of Literature, among other events. Birthplace of composer Gustav Holst.

Cheshire

CHESTER

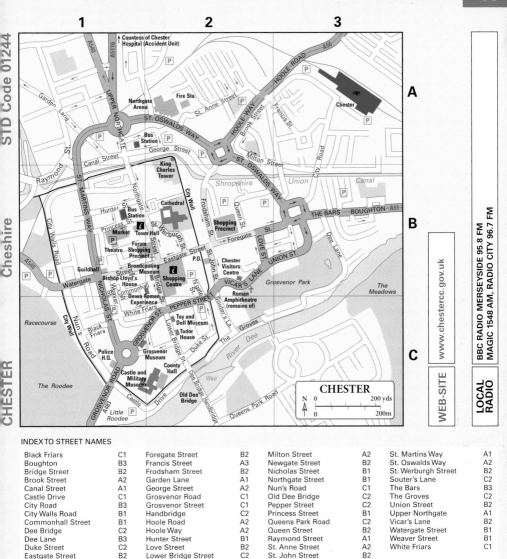

CHESTER

N 0   200 yds

0   200m

WEB-SITE   www.chestercc.gov.uk

LOCAL RADIO   BBC RADIO MERSEYSIDE 95.8 FM   MAGIC 1548 AM, RADIO CITY 96.7 FM

INDEX TO STREET NAMES

TOURIST INFORMATION ☎ 01244 402111
TOWN HALL, NORTHGATE STREET,
CHESTER, CHESHIRE, CH1 2HJ

HOSPITAL A & E ☎ 01244 365000
COUNTESS OF CHESTER HOSPITAL, HEALTH PK,
LIVERPOOL ROAD, CHESTER, CH2 1UL

COUNCIL OFFICE ☎ 01244 324324
THE FORUM,
CHESTER, CH1 2HS

Chester *Ches.* Population: 80110. City, county town and cathedral city on River Dee, 34m/54km SW of Manchester and 15m/24km SE of Birkenhead. Commercial, financial and tourist centre built on Roman town of Deva. Includes biggest Roman amphitheatre in Britain (English Heritage) and well preserved medieval walls (English Heritage). Castle, now county hall, includes 12c Agricola Tower (English Heritage). Cathedral with remains of original Norman abbey. Famed for Tudor timber-framed buildings which include Chester Rows, two-tier galleried shops and Bishop Lloyd's House, with ornate 16c carved façade. Eastgate clock built to commemorate Queen Victoria's diamond jubilee in 1897. Racecourse 1m/2km SW of city centre; zoo 3m/4km N of city centre.

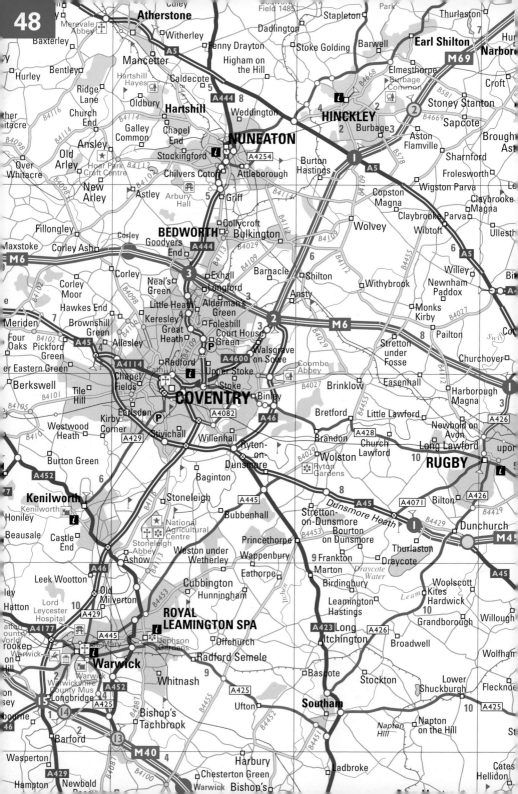

STD Code 024 · West Midlands · COVENTRY

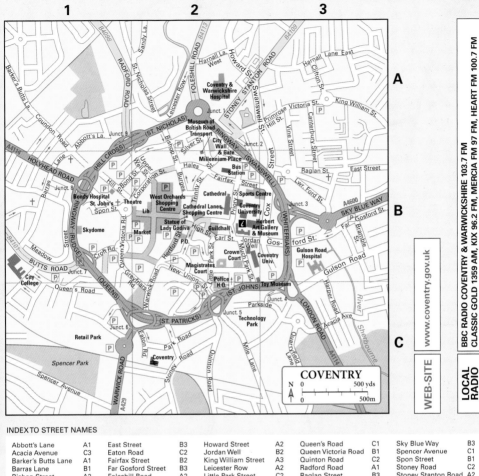

COVENTRY
N 0 ——————— 500 yds
   0 ——————— 500m

INDEX TO STREET NAMES

Coventry *W.Mid.* Population: 299,316. City, 17m/27km E of Birmingham. St. Michael's cathedral built 1954-62 beside ruins of medieval cathedral destroyed in air raid in 1940. The centre of the city was rebuilt in the 1950s and 1960s following WW II bombing, but some old buildings remain, including Bonds Hospital and the medieval Guildhall. A town rich from textile industry in middle ages, Coventry is now known for its motor car industry; other important industries are manufacturing and engineering. Museum of British Road Transport. Herbert Art Gallery and Museum. Universities. Civil airport at Baginton to S. Coventry Canal runs N to Trent and Mersey Canal at Fradley Junction near Lichfield.

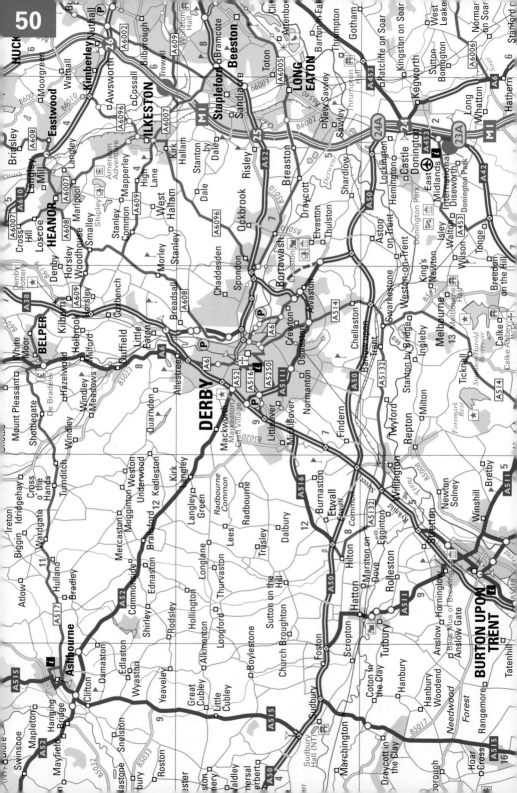

DERBY

SID Code 01332

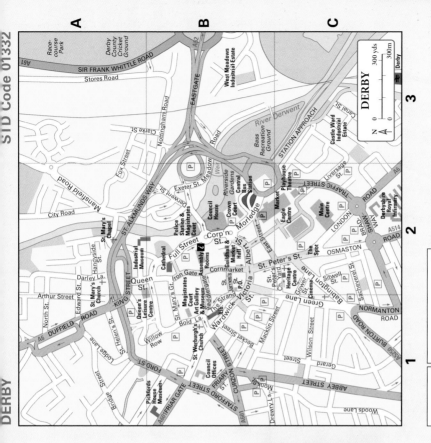

TOURIST INFORMATION ☎ 01332 255802
ASSEMBLY ROOMS, MARKET PLACE,
DERBY, DE1 3AH

HOSPITAL A & E ☎ 01332 347141
DERBYSHIRE ROYAL INFIRMARY,
LONDON ROAD, DERBY, DE1 2QY

COUNCIL OFFICE ☎ 01332 293111
THE COUNCIL HOUSE, CORPORATION STREET,
DERBY, DE1 2FS

Derby Population: 223,836. City, industrial city and county town on River Derwent, 35m/56km NE of Birmingham. Shopping and entertainment centre. Cathedral mainly by James Gibbs, 1725. Both manufacturing and engineering are important to local economy. Derby Industrial Museum charts city's industrial history with emphasis on Rolls Royce aircraft engineering. Tours at Royal Crown Derby porcelain factory. University.

WEB-SITE | www.derby.gov.uk

LOCAL RADIO | BBC RADIO DERBY 104.5 FM
CLASSIC GOLD GEM 945 AM, RAM FM 102.8 FM

South Channel

Long Nose Spit

MARGATE
Dreamland
Foreness Point
White Ness
Tudor House
Westgate on Sea
Cliftonville
Kingsgate
North Foreland
B205
B2052

HERNE BAY
Reculver
Towers & Roman Fort
Birchington
Salmeston Grange
Quex House & Guns
RAF Manston
Spitfire & Hurricane
Memorial Bldg
St Peter's
A255
A254
A256
BROADSTAIRS
Bleak House
Dickens House
A255
A254

Hillborough
Beltinge
Broomfield
Highstead
St Nicholas at Wade
Acol
Isle of Thanet
Manston
A256
A253
RAMSGATE

Hunters Forstal
Boyden Gate
Sarre
Gore Street
Minster
Monkton
Manston
Cliffs End
St Augustine's Cross
Pegwell Bay

Maypole
Hoath
Chislet
Abbey
A28
A256

Herne
Herne mmon
Upstreet
West Stourmouth
Grove
East Stourmouth
Westmarsh
Richborough Castle
Stonar Cut
Great Stonar
Sandwich Flats
Sandwich Bay

cott
A291
Roman Road
Stodmarsh
Hersden
Preston
Ware
Cop Street
Elmstone
Roman Amphitheatre
Sandwich
Salutation Gdn
Toll

turry
dwich
Great Stour
Westbere
Stodmarsh
Hoaden
Bird Park
Great Stour
Wickhambreaux
Ickham
Ash
Marshborough
Worth
Hacklinge

RBURY
2050
A257
Littlebourne
Howletts Wild Animal Park
Wingham
Staple
Woodnesborough
Ham
Worth
A258

ustine's Abbey
Bramling
Bekesbourne
Goodnestone Park
Goodnestone
Eastry
Finglesham
Betteshanger
Sholden
DEAL

Patrixbourne
Chillenden
Knowlton
Deal

Bridge
A2
Adisham
Nonington
Tilmanstone
A256
Northbourne
Great Mongeham
Walmer

Hardres
psbourne
Aylesham
Easole Street
Elvington
East Studdal
Ripple
Sutton
Walmer Castle & Garden
Kingsdown

Kingston
Barham
Womenswold
Barfreston
Eythorne
Ashley
West Langdon
Ringwould
A258

Derringstone
Woollage Green
Shepherdswell (Sibertswold)
Coldred
East Langdon
Martin Mill Sta.
A258

inge Forest
Breach
Denton
Lydden
Wootton
Lydden
A2
Whitfield
Guston
West Cliffe
St Margaret's at Cliffe

Elham
Bladbean
Wingmore
Selstead
A260
Temple Ewell
St Margaret's Bay
The Pines

Acrise Place
Swingfield Minnis
Ewell Minnis
Alkham
Buckland
South Foreland

ttinge
Lyminge
Densole
St Radigund's Abbey
Dover
DOVER

Paddlesworth
Hawkinge
Drellingore
West Hougham
Maxton
De Bradelei Wharf

Etchinghill
192
West Hougham
Farthingloe
Knights Templar Church

Newington
Channel Tunnel Terminal
Capel le Ferne
B2011
East Wear Bay
Channel Tunnel
Calais..................
Oostende..............
Zeebrugge............

11A
12
13
Cheriton
A20
FOLKESTONE

A259
Sandgate
Rotunda Amusement Park
Hythe

A299
A28
A253
A256
A257
A2
A20
A260

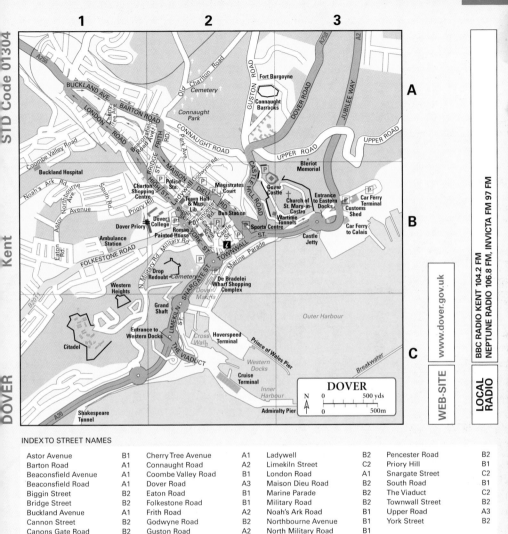

Kent

DOVER

WEB-SITE www.dover.gov.uk

LOCAL RADIO BBC RADIO KENT 104.2 FM / NEPTUNE RADIO 106.8 FM, INVICTA FM 97 FM

DOVER
N 0 ——— 500 yds
   0 ——— 500m

INDEX TO STREET NAMES

TOURIST INFORMATION ☎ 01304 205108
TOWNWALL STREET,
DOVER, KENT, CT16 1JR

HOSPITAL A & E ☎ 01227 766877
KENT & CANTERBURY HOSPITAL,
ETHELBERT ROAD, CANTERBURY, CT1 3NG

COUNCIL OFFICE ☎ 01304 821199
WHITE CLIFFS BUSINESS PARK,
DOVER, CT16 3PJ

Dover *Kent* Population: 34,179. Town, cinque port, resort and Channel port on Strait of Dover, 15m/24km SE of Canterbury, with large modern docks for freight and passengers. Dominated by high white cliffs and medieval castle (English Heritage) enclosing the Pharos, 50AD remains of Roman lighthouse. Remains of 12c Knights Templar Church (English Heritage) across valley from castle. Sections of moat of 19c fort at Western Heights (English Heritage), above town on W side of harbour. White Cliffs Experience re-creates Roman and wartime Dover.

DUNDEE

Carnoustie
Monifieth
Tayport
Newport-on-Tay
Leuchars
Guardbridge
Kincaple
Newburgh
Coupar Angus
Rattray
Blairgowrie

Arbirlot
Guynd
Carmyllie
Greystone
Bonnyton
Mosston
Lochlair
Tulloes
Lochlair
Hayillock
Kirkbuddo
Whigstreet
Inverarity
Kincaldrum
Gateside
Gallowfauld
Carrot
Carrot Hill
Todhills
Balgray
Kirkton of Monikie
Newton of Affleck
Affleck
Monikie
Greenburn
Bucklerheads
Wellbank
Newbigging East March
Kellas
Baldovie
Murroes
Burnside of Duntrune
Douglas and Angus
Upper Victoria
Muirdrum
Craigton
Mains of Ardestie
Barry
Buddon
Barry Links
Buddon Ness
Tentsmuir Point
Tentsmuir
Forest
RAF Memorial
Earlshall
Eden Mouth
Out Head
St Andrews Golf Bay
British Golf Museum
Pickletillem
Carrick
Cruivie
Balmullo
Logie
Lucklawhill
Dairsie
Woodhaven
Wormit
Kirkton
Bottomcraig
Gauldry
Rathillet
Craigsanquhar
Kilmany
Forret Hill
Hazelton Walls
Brunton
Creich
Luthrie
Balhelvie
Coultra
Balmerino
Moonzie
Norman's Law
Glenduckie Hill
Glenduckie
Dunbog
Lindores Abbey
Mugdrum Island
Port Allen
Errol
Glencarse
Chapelhill
Inchyra
Pole Hill
Kinfauns Forest
Glendoick
Pitroddie
Kilspindie
Rait
Grange
Inchture
Longforgan
Kingoodie
Invergowrie
Kinnaird
Megginch Castle
Craigdallie
Ballindean
Knapp
Abernyte
Rossie Priory
Littleton
Blacklaw Hill
King's Seat
Pitmiddle Wood
Fowlis
Benvie
Liff
Camperdown
Muirhead
Birkhill
Dronley
Auchterhouse
Leoch
Leys
Pitcur
Kettins
Markethill
Campmuir
Burrelton
Woodside
Kinrossie
Kirkton of Collace
Collace
Saucher
Springfield
Whitefield
Keithick
Rosemount
Kinloch
Ardler
Arthurstone
Newbigging
Auchtertyre
Newtyle
Meigle
Balkeerie
Kirkinch
Eassie and Nevay
Nether Handwick
Kinpurney Hill
Auchterhouse Hill
Craigowl Hill
Gallow Hill
Kirkton of Tealing
Dovecot & Earth House
Kirkton of Strathmartine
Clatto
Downfield
Denhead
Lochee
Kingsway
Discovery Point & R.R.S. Discovery
Broughty Ferry
Broughty
Tay Road Bridge
Tay Bridge
Dog Bank
Carthagena Bank
Norman's Law
Brae s of the Carse
Gowrie

A90 A92 A85 A923 A928 A930 A914 A919 A913 A984 A94 B9127 B9128 B961 B945 B946 B954 B953

FIRTH OF TAY

DUNDEE

STD Code 01382

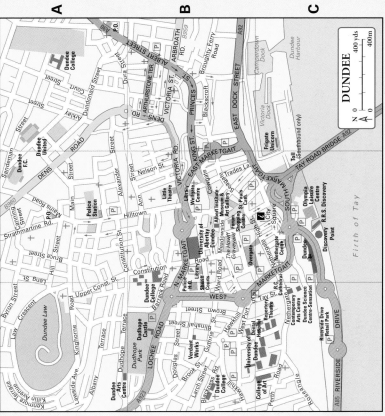

INDEX TO STREET NAMES

Albany Terrace	A1	Dens Road	A2
Albert Street	B3	Douglas Street	B1
Alexander Street	A2	Dudhope Terrace	A1
Ann Street	B2	Dudhope Terrace	A1
Arbroath Road	C1	Dundonald Street	A2
Arklay Street	A3	Dura Street	A3
Arthurstone	B3	East Dock Street	B3
Terrace		East Marketgait	B2
Barrack Road	B1	Guthrie Street	B1
Blackness Road	B1	Hawkhill	B1
Blackscroft	B3	High Street	B2
Blinshall Street	B1	Hill Street	B1
Brook Street	B1	Hilltown	A2
Broughty Ferry	B3	Kenmore Terrace	A1
Road		Killin Avenue	A1
Brown Street	B1	Kinghorne Road	A1
Bruce Street	A1	King Street	B2
Byron Street	A1	Larch Street	B1
Canning Street	A2	Law Crescent	A1
City Square	C2	Lawside Avenue	A1
Constitution Road	B2	Leng Street	A2
Constitution Street	A3	Lochee Road	B1
Court Street	A3	Mains Road	A2
Cowgate Street	B2	Main Street	A2

Meadowside	B2
Nelson Street	B2
North Marketgait	C1
Perth Road	C1
Princes Street	B3
Roseangle	C1
Riverside Drive	C1
Seagate	B2
South Marketgait	C2
South Tay Street	C1
Strathmartine	A2
Road	
Tay Road Bridge	C2
Trades Lane	B2
Upper Constitution	A1
Street	
Victoria Road	B2
Victoria Street	B3
Ward Road	B1
West Marketgait	B1
West Port	B1

TOURIST INFORMATION ☎ 01382 527527
21 CASTLE STREET,
DUNDEE, DD1 3BA

HOSPITAL A & E ☎ 01382 660111
NINEWELLS HOSPITAL, NINEWELLS ROAD,
DUNDEE, DD1 9SY

COUNCIL OFFICE ☎ 01382 434000
CITY CHAMBERS, 21 CITY SQUARE,
DUNDEE, DD1 3BY

Dundee Population: 158,981. City, Scotland's fourth largest city, commercial and industrial centre and port, 18m/29km E of Perth on N side of Firth of Tay, crossed here by a 1m/2km road bridge and a 2m/3km railway bridge. Robert the Bruce declared King of the Scots in Dundee in 1309. Sustained severe damage during Civil War and again prior to Jacobite uprising. City recovered in early 19c and became Britain's main processor of jute. One of largest employers in Dundee today is D.C. Thomson, publisher of The Beano and The Dandy. Many museums and art galleries. Cultural centre, occasionally playing host to former castle. Universities. Ship 'Discovery' in which Captain Scott travelled to Antarctic has returned to Victoria dock, where she was built.

WEB-SITE   www.dundeecity.gov.uk

LOCAL RADIO   BBC RADIO SCOTLAND 810 AM/92.4-94.7 FM
TAY AM 1161 AM, WAVE 102 FM, TAY FM 102.8 FM

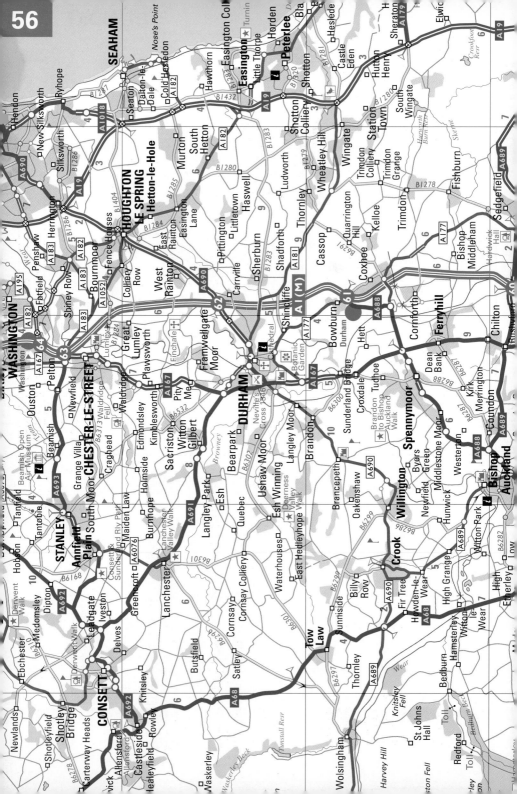

STD Code 0191

DURHAM

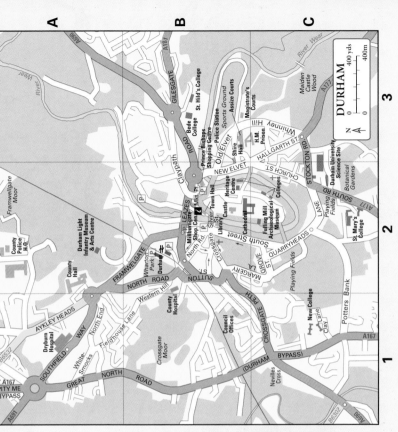

TOURIST INFORMATION ☎ 0191 384 3720
MARKET PLACE, DURHAM,
COUNTY DURHAM, DH1 3NJ

HOSPITAL A & E ☎ 0191 333 2333
DRYBURN HOSPITAL, NORTH ROAD,
DURHAM, DH1 5TW

COUNCIL OFFICE ☎ 0191 386 4411
COUNTY HALL,
DURHAM, DH1 5UB

Durham *Dur.* Population: 36,937. Cathedral city on narrow bend in River Wear, 14m/22km S of Newcastle upon Tyne. Norman-Romanesque cathedral founded in 1093 on site of shrine of St. Cuthbert is World Heritage Site. England's third oldest University founded in 1832. Motteand-bailey castle dating from 1072 now part of the University. Collection in Fulling Mill Museum of Archaelogy illustrates history of city. Museum of Oriental Art. Light Infantry Museum. Art Gallery. University Botanic Garden S of city.

WEB-SITE www.durhamcity.gov.uk

LOCAL RADIO BBC RADIO NEWCASTLE 95.4 FM
SUN FM 103.4 FM, GALAXY 105-106 105.3, 105.6, 105.8 & 106.4 FM

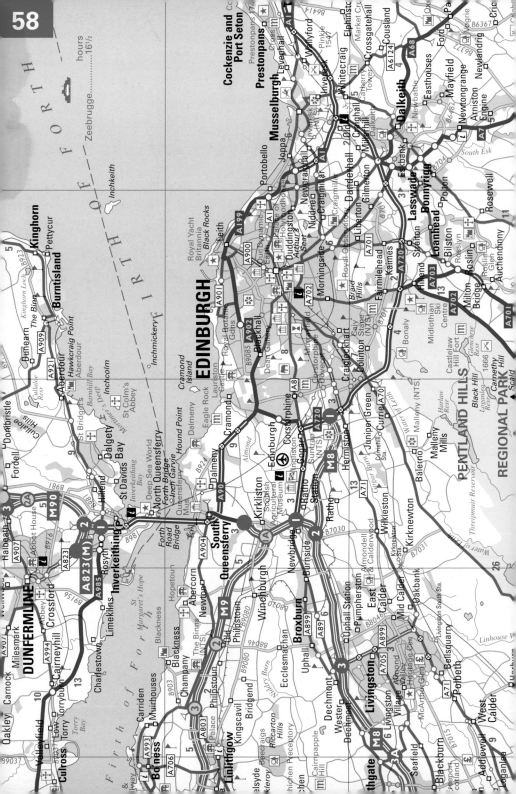

EDINBURGH

STD Code 0131

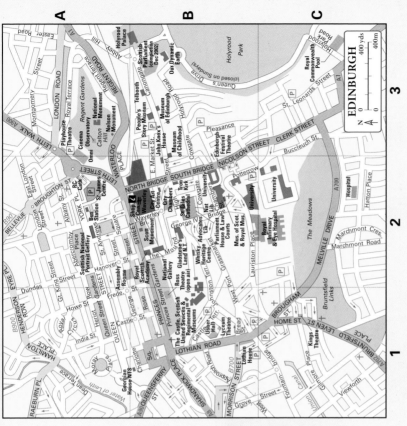

INDEX TO STREET NAMES

TOURIST INFORMATION ☎ 0131 473 3800
**INFORMATION CENTRE, 3 PRINCES STREET,
EDINBURGH, EH2 2QP**

HOSPITAL A & E ☎ 0131 536 1000
**ROYAL INFIRMARY OF EDINBURGH,
1 LAURISTON PLACE, EDINBURGH, EH3 9YW**

COUNCIL OFFICE ☎ 0131 200 2000
**COUNCIL HEADQUARTERS, 10 WATERLOO PLACE,
EDINBURGH, EH1 3EG**

WEB-SITE www.edinburgh.gov.uk

LOCAL RADIO BBC RADIO SCOTLAND 810 AM & 92.4-94.7 FM
FORTH 2 1548 AM, FORTH ONE 97.3 FM, REAL RADIO 101.1 FM

Edinburgh *Edin.* Population: 401,910. City, historic city and capital of Scotland, built on a range of rocky crags and extinct volcanoes, on S side of Firth of Forth, 41m/66km E of Glasgow. Administrative, financial and legal centre of Scotland. Medieval castle (Historic Scotland) on rocky eminence overlooks central area and was one of main seats of Royal court, while universities. Port at Leith, where Royal Yacht Britannia is now docked and open to public. Important industries include brewing, distilling, food and electronics. Palace of Holyroodhouse (Historic Scotland) is chief royal residence of Scotland. Old Town typified by Gladstone's Land (Historic Scotland). 17c six-storey tenement with arcaded front, outside stair and stepped gables. Numerous literary associations including Sir Arthur Conan Doyle who was born here. Many galleries and museums including National Gallery of Scotland. Annual arts festival attracts over a million visitors each year and is largest such event in the world.

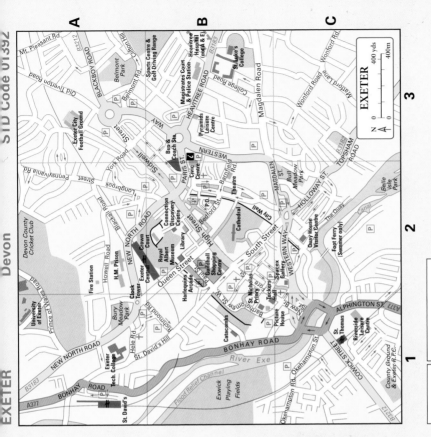

TOURIST INFORMATION ☎ 01392 265700
CIVIC CENTRE, PARIS STREET, EXETER,
DEVON, EX1 1RP

HOSPITAL A & E ☎ 01392 411611
ROYAL DEVON & EXETER HOSPITAL (WONFORD),
BARRACK ROAD, EXETER, EX2 5DW

COUNCIL OFFICE ☎ 01392 277888
CIVIC CENTRE, PARIS STREET,
EXETER, EX1 1JN

Exeter *Devon* Population: 94,717. City, county capital on River Exe, 64m/103km SW of Bristol. Major administrative, business and financial centre on site of Roman town Isca Dumnoniorum. Cathedral is Decorated, with Norman towers and façade with hundreds of stone statues. 15c guildhall. Modern buildings in centre built after extensive damage from World War II. Beneath the city lie remains of medieval water-supply system built in 14c to supply fresh water to city centre. Royal Albert Memorial Museum and Art Gallery. Early 16c mansion of Bowhill (English Heritage), with preserved Great Hall, 2m/3km SW. University 1m/2km N of city centre. Airport 5m/8km E at Clyst Honiton.

WEB-SITE www.exeter.gov.uk

LOCAL RADIO BBC RADIO DEVON 95.8 FM
CLASSIC GOLD 666 AM, GEMINI FM 97 & 103 FM

FOLKESTONE   **Kent**   **STD Code 01303**

FOLKESTONE

N

0   200 yds
0   200m

INDEX TO STREET NAMES

Alder Road	B2	Hill Road	A3
Bathurst Road	B1	Joyes Road	A3
Black Bull Road	B2	Links Way	A1
Bournemouth Road	B2	Lower Sandgate Road	C1
Bouverie Road West	C1	Lucy Avenue	A1
Bradstone Road	B2	Manor Road	C2
Broadmead Road	B2	Marine Parade	C2
Canterbury Road	A3	Park Farm Road	A2
Castle Hill Avenue	C2	Pavilion Road	B2
Cheriton Gardens	C2	Radnor Bridge Road	B3
Cheriton Road	B1	Radnor Park Avenue	B1
Cherry Garden Avenue	A1	Radnor Park Road	B2
Churchill Avenue	A2	Radnor Park West	B1
Coniston Road	A1	Sandgate Hill	C1
Coolinge Road	B2	Sandgate Road	C2
Cornwallis Avenue	A2	Shorncliffe Road	B1
Dolphins Road	A3	Sidney Street	B3
Dover Road	A3	The Leas	C2
Downs Road	A2	The Stade	C3
Earles Avenue	C1	The Tram Raod	B3
Foord Road	B2	Tontine Street	B3
Grimston Avenue	C1	Turketel Road	C1
Guildhall Street	B2	Wear Bay Crescent	B3
Guildhall Street North	B2	Wear Bay Road	A3
Harbour Way	B3	Wood Avenue	A3
High Street	B1	Wilton Road	C3

TOURIST INFORMATION ☎ 01303 258594
HARBOUR STREET, FOLKESTONE,
KENT, CT20 1QN

HOSPITAL A & E ☎ 01233 633331
WILLIAM HARVEY HOSPITAL, KENNINGTON RD,
WILLESBOROUGH, ASHFORD, TN24 0LZ

COUNCIL OFFICE ☎ 01303 850388
CIVIC CENTRE, CASTLE HILL AVENUE,
FOLKESTONE, CT20 2QY

Folkestone *Kent* Population: 45,587. Town, Channel port and resort, 14m/22km E of Ashford. Russian submarine docked in harbour is open to the public. The Lear marine promenade accessed by Victorian cliff lift. Ornate Victorian hotels. Martello tower on East Cliff. Kent Battle of Britain Museum at Hawkinge airfield 3m/5km N. Channel Tunnel terminal on N side.

WEB-SITE   www.shepway.gov.uk

LOCAL RADIO   BBC RADIO KENT 97.6 FM   INVICTA FM 97 FM

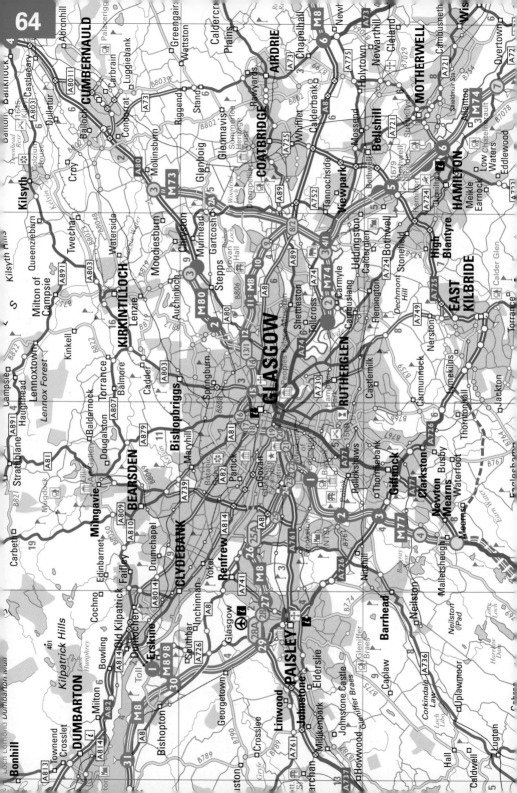

GLASGOW

STD Code 0141

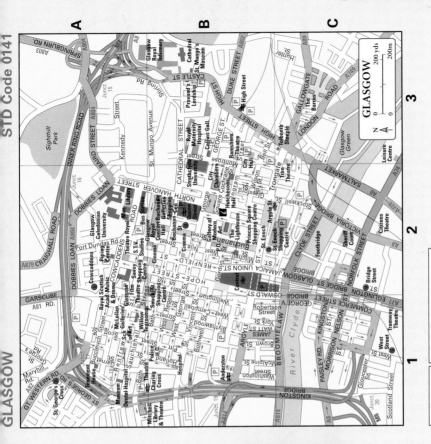

INDEX TO STREET NAMES

Argyle Street	B1
Baird Street	A3
Bath Street	A1/B1
Bell Street	B3
Blythswood Street	B1
Bothwell Street	B1
Bridge Street	C2
Broomielaw	C1
Brown Street	B1
Buccleuch Street	A1
Buchanan Street	B2
Castle Street	A3
Cathedral Street	B2
Clyde Street	C1
Cochrane Street	B2
Commerce Street	C1
Cowcaddens Road	A2
Craighall Road	A2
Dobbie's Loan	A2
Duke Street	B3
Eglinton Street	C1
Gallowgate	C3
Garnet Street	A1
Garscube Road	A1
George Square	B2
George Street	B3
George V Bridge	C1
Glasgow Bridge	C2
Glassford Street	B2
Gloucester Street	C1
Gordon Street	B2
Great Western Road	A1
High Street	B3
Holland Street	B1
Hope Street	B2
Hunter Street	B3
Ingram Street	B2
Inner Ring Road	B2
Jamaica Street	C2
James Watt Street	C1
Kennedy Street	A3
Kingston Bridge	C1
Kingston Street	C1
London Road	C3
Maryhill Road	A1
McAlpine Street	C1
Mitchell Street	B2
Montrose Street	B2
Morrison Street	C1
Nelson Street	C1
Norfolk Street	C1
North Hanover Street	B2
Oswald Street	C1
Paisley Road	C1
Pitt Street	B1
Port Dundas Road	A2
Renfield Street	B2
Renfrew Street	A1
Robertson Street	C1
Saltmarket	C3
Scotland Street	C1
Scott Street	A1
Springburn Road	A3
St. George's Road	A1
St. Mungo Avenue	B3
St. Vincent Street	B1
Stirling Road	B3
Stockwell Street	C2
Trongate	C2
Union Street	B2
Victoria Bridge	C2
Washington Street	C1
Wellington Street	B1
West Campbell Street	B1
West George Street	B1
West Nile Street	B2
West Regent Street	B1
West Street	C1
Wilson Street	B2
York Street	C1

TOURIST INFORMATION ☎ 0141 204 4400
11 GEORGE SQUARE,
GLASGOW, G2 1DY

HOSPITAL A & E ☎ 0141 211 2000
WESTERN INFIRMARY, DUMBARTON ROAD,
GLASGOW, G11 6NT

COUNCIL OFFICE ☎ 0141 287 2000
CITY CHAMBERS, GEORGE SQUARE,
GLASGOW, G2 1DU

Glasgow *Glas.* Population: 662,954. City, largest city in Scotland. Port and commercial, industrial, cultural and entertainment centre on River Clyde, 41m/66km W of Edinburgh and 346m/557km NW of London. Major industrial port and important trading point with America until War of Independence. During industrial revolution, nearby coal seams boosted Glasgow's importance and its population increased ten-fold between 1800 and 1900. By beginning of 20c shipbuilding dominated the city, although industry went into decline in 1930's. Glasgow is now seen to be a city of culture and progress. It has a strong performing arts tradition and many museums and galleries including Burrell Collection (set in Pollok Country Park). Cathedral is rare example of an almost complete 13c church. Early 19c Hutcheson's Hall (National Trust for Scotland) in Ingram Street is one of city's most elegant buildings; Tenement House (National Trust for Scotland) is late Victorian tenement flat retaining many original features. Three universities. Airport 7m/11km W.

WEB-SITE www.glasgow.gov.uk

LOCAL RADIO BBC RADIO SCOTLAND 810 AM & 92.4-94.7 FM
CLYDE 1 102.5 FM, CLYDE 2 1152 AM, REAL RADIO 100.3 FM

CHELTENHAM

Charlton
Kings

CIRENCESTER

Cirencester

Winchcombe

Bishop's
Cleeve

GLOUCESTER

STROUD

COTSWOLD HILLS

VALE OF GLOUCESTER

Newent

Cinderford

M5
M50

A40
A417
A419
A429
A436
A435
A46
A38
A48
A430
A4173
A4019
A417

Charlton Abbots
Hawling
Charlton Abbots
Sudeley
Isbourne
Belas Knap Long Barrow
Roman Villa
Brockhampton
Sevenhampton
Syreford
Shipton
Compton Abdale
Withington
Withington Woods
Chedworth
Chedworth Roman Villa (NT)
Chedworth Woods
Yanworth
Fossebridge
Foss Cross
Calmsden
Barnsley
St John Baptist Church

Southam
Cleeve Hill
Prestbury
Dowdeswell
Whittington
Arlecenford
Kilkenny
Colesbourne
Rendcomb
North Cerney
Woodmancote
Baunton
Stratton
Corinium Amphitheatre

Woodmancote
Swindon
Elmstone Hardwicke
Uckington Village
Hatherley
Up Hatherley
Pilley
Leckhampton
Shurdington
Bentham
Crickley Hill
Little Witcombe
Great Witcombe
Cranham
Brimpsfield
Caudle Green
Whiteway
The Camp
Syde
Winstone
Misarden
Misarden Park Gardens
Sudgrove
Duntisbourne Abbots
Edgeworth
Oakridge Lynch
Daglingworth
Sapperton
Frampton Mansell
Bourne's Green
Chalford
Bisley
Eastcombe
Bussage
Brimscombe
Thrupp
Rodborough
Woodchester

Seven Springs
Upper Coberley
Coberley
Cowley
Elkstone
Cobley
Birdlip
Brimpsfield

Staverton
Staverton Bridge
Churchdown
Badgeworth
Brockworth
Hucclecote
Barnwood
Matson
Upton St Leonards
Prinknash Abbey
Prinknash Pottery
Cranham
Sheepscombe
Slad
Painswick
Edge
Pitchcombe
Harescombe
Brookthorpe
Rococo
Whiteshill
Randwick

Innsworth
Longford
Twigworth
Longlevens
Hempstead
Tuffley
Whaddon
Robinswood Hill
Harescombe
Haresfield
Stroud Green
Stonehouse
Leonard Stanley
King's Stanley
Woodchester

Maisemore
Sandhurst
Ashleworth
Ashleworth Tithe Barn (NT)
Hartpury
Highleadon
Rudford
Tibberton
Taynton
Huntley
Bulley
Churcham
Minsterworth
Elmore Back
Elmore
Farleys End
Hardwicke
Quedgeley
Moreton Valence
Longney
Putloe
Whitminster
Eastington
Frocester
Leonard Stanley
Coaley
Cambridge
Slimbridge

Ashleworth
White End
Hasfield
Nup End
Corse
Apperley
Lower Apperley
Tirley
Hartpury
Blackwells End
Coombe Hill
Boddington
Stoke Orchard
Hardwicke
Elmstone Hardwicke

Frampton on Severn
Saul
Wheatenhurst
Upper Framilode
Framilode
Rodley
Westbury-on-Severn
Westbury Court (NT)
Flaxley
Boxbush
Northwood Green
Oakle Street
Birdwood
Glasshouse Hill
Huntley
Longhope
Harts Barn Craft Centre
May Hill
Clifford's Mesne
Aston Ingham
Little Gorsley
Gorsley
Gorsley Common
Kempley
Kempley Green
Brand Green
Botloe's Green
Upleadon
Kent's Green

Mitcheldean
Littledean
Littledean Hall
Dean Heritage Centre
Ruspidge
Upper Soudley
Blaisdon
Flaxley
Elton
Newnham
Arlingham
Awre
The Noose
Blakeney
Viney Hill
Nibley
Purton
Sharpness
New Grounds
Slimbridge

Bromsash
Lea
Aston Crews
Upton Bishop
Kempley Church

B4213
B4215
B4216
B4224
B4063
B4061
B4008
B4071
B4073
B4088
B4010
B4070
A4136
A4151
A4222
A435
A436
A417
A419

GLOUCESTER · Gloucestershire · STD Code 01452

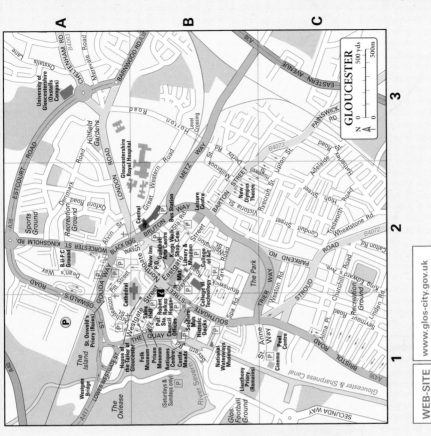

GLOUCESTER
N
0   500 yds
0   500m

INDEX TO STREET NAMES

Adelaide Street	C2	Greyfriars	B2
Alma Place	C1	Hatherley Road	C2
Alvin Street	A2	High Street	C1
Archdeacon Street	A1	Hopewell Street	C2
Barnwood Road	A3	Horton Road	B3
Barton Street	B2	King Edward's	C2
Bristol Road	A2	Avenue	
Brunswick Road	C1	Kingsholm Road	A2
Bruton Way	B2	Linden Road	C1
Calton Road	C2	London Road	A2
Cheltenham Road	A3	Lower Westgate	A1
Churchill Road	C1	Street	
Conduit Street	C2	Merevale Road	A3
Dean's Way	A2	Metz Way	B2
Denmark Road	A2	Millbrook Street	B2
Derby Road	B2	Northgate Street	A2
Estcourt Road	A2	Oxford Road	A3
Eastern Avenue	C3	Oxstalls Lane	A3
Eastgate Street	B2	Painswick Road	C3
Gouda Way	A1	Park Road	B2
Great Western	B2	Parkend Road	C2
Road		Pitt Street	A2
		Quay Street	B1
Ryecroft Street	C2		
St. Ann Way	C1		
St. Oswald's Road	A1		
Secunda Way	C2		
Severn Road	B1		
Seymour Road	C2		
Southgate Street	B1		
Spa Road	B1		
Station Road	B2		
Stroud Road	C1		
The Quay	B1		
Tredworth Road	C2		
Trier Way	C1		
Upton Street	C2		
Victoria Street	B2		
Wellington Street	B2		
Westgate Street	A1		
Weston Road	C1		
Wheatstone Road	C2		
Worcester Street	A2		

TOURIST INFORMATION ☎ 01452 421188
28 SOUTHGATE STREET, GLOUCESTER,
GLOUCESTERSHIRE, GL1 2DP

HOSPITAL A & E ☎ 01452 528555
GLOUCESTER ROYAL HOSPITAL
GREAT WESTERN RD, GLOUCESTER, GL1 3NN

COUNCIL OFFICE ☎ 01452 522232
COUNCIL OFFICES, NORTH WAREHOUSE,
THE DOCKS, GLOUCESTER, GL1 2EP

Gloucester *Glos.* Population: 114,003. City, industrial city on River Severn, on site of Roman town of Glevum, 32m/52km NE of Bristol. Norman era saw Gloucester grow in political importance, from here William the Conqueror ordered survey of his Kingdom which resulted in Domesday Book of 1086. City became a religious centre during middle ages. Cathedral built in mixture of Norman and Perpendicular styles, has cloisters and England's largest stained glass window, dating from 14c. Remains of 15c-16c Franciscan friary, Greyfriars, (English Heritage). Historic docks, now largely redeveloped, on Gloucester and Sharpness Canal. Three Choirs Festival held every third year.

WEB-SITE   www.glos-city.gov.uk

LOCAL RADIO   BBC RADIO GLOUCESTERSHIRE 104.7 FM
CLASSIC GOLD 774 AM, SEVERN SOUND FM 102.4 & 103 FM

Shirl Heath · Cobnash · Eyton · Stockton · Whyle · Grafton · Collington · High Lane · Wolferlow

Lawton · Cholstrey · Bach Camp · Hatfield · Thornbury · Wall Hills · Edvin Loach

Leominster · Steen's Bridge · Pudleston · Grendon Green · Edwyn Ralph

Burton Court · Strefford Court · Monkland · Stoke Prior · Humber · Docklow · 11 · Bredenbury · Bromyard Downs · Broc

Arrow · Ivington · Ivington Green · Wharton · Risbury · **Bromyard**

Dilwyn Common · Brierley · Aulden · Marston Stannett

Dilwyn · Upper Hill · Hope under Dinmore · Bowley · 11 · Pencombe · Little Cowarne · Munderfield Row · Stan Bish

Knapton Green · Birley · Bush Bank · Queenswood · Bodenham · Maund Bryan · Ullingswick · Munderfield Stocks · Acton Beauc

Weobley Marsh · King's Pyon · Westhope · Dinmore Manor · Bodenham Moor · The Vauld · Felton · Stoke Lacy · Bishop's Frome

Canon Pyon · Urdimarsh · Walker's Green · Preston Wynne · Burley Gate · Moreton Jeffries

Wormsley · Yarsop · Foxley · Tillington Common · Wellington · Wellington Marsh · Marden · Sutton Walls · Ocle Pychard · Much Cowarne · Five Bridges

Mansell Lacy · Tillington · Brinsop · Burghill · Moreton on Lugg · Sutton St Nicholas · 7 · Newtown · Lower Egleton · Castle Frome

Bishopstone · Credenhill · Stretton Sugwas · Pipe and Lyde · Shelwick · Westhide · Stretton Grandison · Canon Frome

Kenchester · Holmer · Withington · Yarkhill · Ashperton

The Weir (NT) · Canon Bridge · Swainshill · Hereford · Shucknall · Hagley · Weston · Tarrington · Trumpet

Upper Breinton · White Cross · **HEREFORD** · Lugwardine · Bartestree · Beggard · Dormington · 10

Breinton · Cath · Tupsley · Prior's Frome · Muns

Eaton Bishop · Belmont Abbey · Lower Bullingham · Rotherwas Chapel · Hampton Bishop · Checkley · Aylton · Putley

Madley · Clehonger · Grafton · Dinedor · Holme Lacy · Mordiford · Fiddler's Green · Little Marcle

Kingstone · Allensmore · Dinedor · Twyford Common · Fownhope · Woolhope · Rushall

Thruxton · Whitfield · Didley · Callow · Dewsall Court · St. John Baptist · Aconbury · Bolstone · Ballingham · Sollers Hope · Much Marcle · Tillers

Howton · Kilpeck · Much Dewchurch · Wormelow Tump · Kingsthorne · Little Birch · Little Dewchurch · Carey · Brockhampton · Hellen's

Kenderchurch · Bagwyllydiart · Orcop Hill · Much Birch · Penalt · Fawley Chapel · How Caple · Yatton Wood · Old Gore

Kentchurch · Garway Hill · Llanwarne · Pencoyd · Hoarwithy · Llandinabo · Harewood End · Kings Caple · Baysham · Hole-in-the-Wall · Upton Bishop · Kem Gree

Orcop · Sandyway · Michaelchurch · Sellack · Brampton Abbotts · Crow Hill · Gorsle

Little Garway · St Owen's Cross · Tretire · Peterstow · Bridstow · Ross Spur · Rudhall · Linton · Little Gors

Garway · St Weonards · Hom Green · **Ross-on-Wye** · Weston under Penyard · Bromsash · Aston Crews

Skenfrith (NT) · Llangarron · Glewstone · Hillcourt · Coughton · Pontshill · Lea

Broad Oak · Pencraig

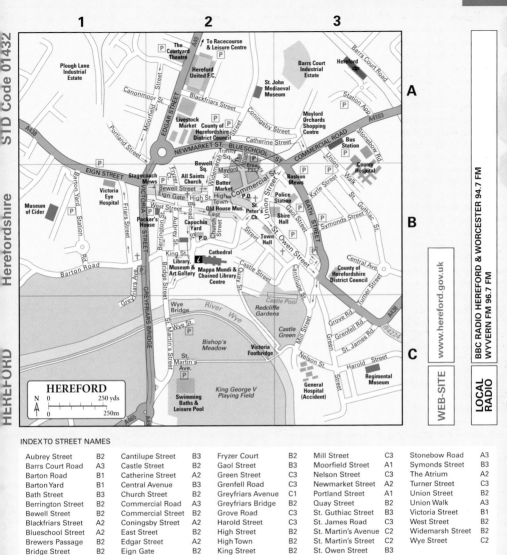

STD Code 01432

Herefordshire

HEREFORD

WEB-SITE www.hereford.gov.uk

LOCAL RADIO BBC RADIO HEREFORD & WORCESTER 94.7 FM WYVERN FM 96.7 FM

INDEX TO STREET NAMES

TOURIST INFORMATION ☎ 01432 268430
1 KING STREET,
HEREFORD, HR4 9BW

HOSPITAL A & E ☎ 01432 355444
HEREFORD GENERAL HOSPITAL,
NELSON STREET, HEREFORD, HR1 2PA

COUNCIL OFFICE ☎ 01432 260456
COUNCIL OFFICES, THE TOWN HALL,
HEREFORD, HR1 2PJ

Hereford *Here.* Population: 54,326. City, county town and cathedral city on River Wye, 45m/72km SW of Birmingham. Many old buildings and museums, including Waterworks museum and City Museum and Art Gallery. 1621 Old House is a museum of local history. Medieval Wye Bridge. Cathedral includes richly ornamented Early English style Lady chapel. New building houses Chained Library of 1500 volumes and 1289 Mappa Mundi Map of the world. Three Choirs Festival every third year. Cider Museum and King Offa Distillery W of city centre depicts history of cider making.

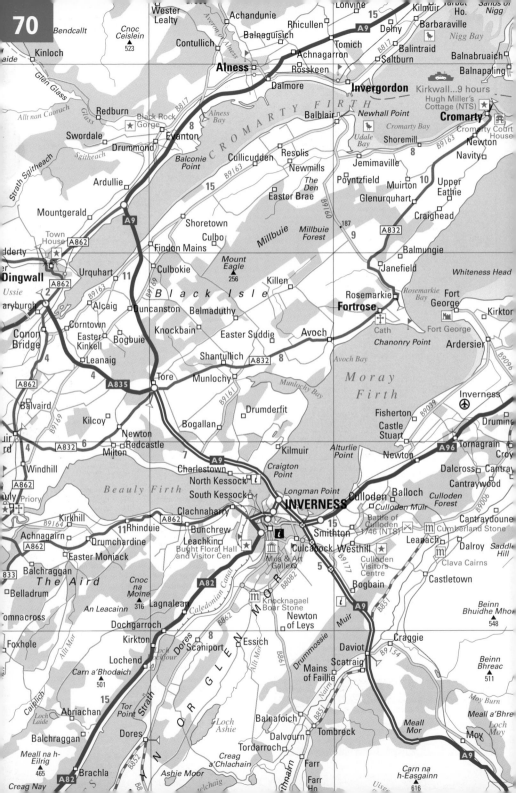

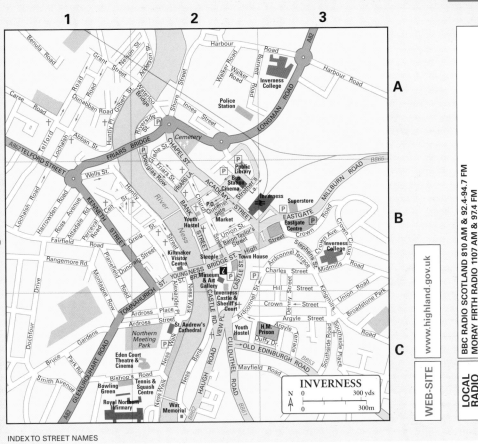

INVERNESS

N 0   300 yds

0   300m

**TOURIST INFORMATION ☎ 01463 234353
CASTLE WYND,
INVERNESS, HIGHLAND, IV2 3BJ**

**HOSPITAL A & E ☎ 01463 704000
RAIGMORE HOSPITAL, OLD PERTH ROAD,
INVERNESS, IV2 3UJ**

**COUNCIL OFFICE ☎ 01463 702000
COUNCIL OFFICES, GLENURQUHART ROAD,
INVERNESS, IV3 5NX**

Inverness *High.* Population: 41,234. Town, at mouth of River Ness at entrance to Beauly Firth, 105m/169km NW of Aberdeen and 113m/181km NW of Edinburgh. Administrative, commercial and tourist centre. Caledonian Canal passes to W of town. Victorian castle in town centre used as law courts. Inverness Museum and Art Gallery depicts history of Highlands. Balnain House is a museum of Highland music and musical instruments. University of the Highlands and Islands. 1746 Culloden battle site 5m/8km E. Airport at locality of Dalcross, 7m/11km NE of town.

STD Code 01463   Highland   INVERNESS

www.highland.gov.uk   WEB-SITE

BBC RADIO SCOTLAND 810 AM & 92.4-94.7 FM
MORAY FIRTH RADIO 1107 AM & 97.4 FM   LOCAL RADIO

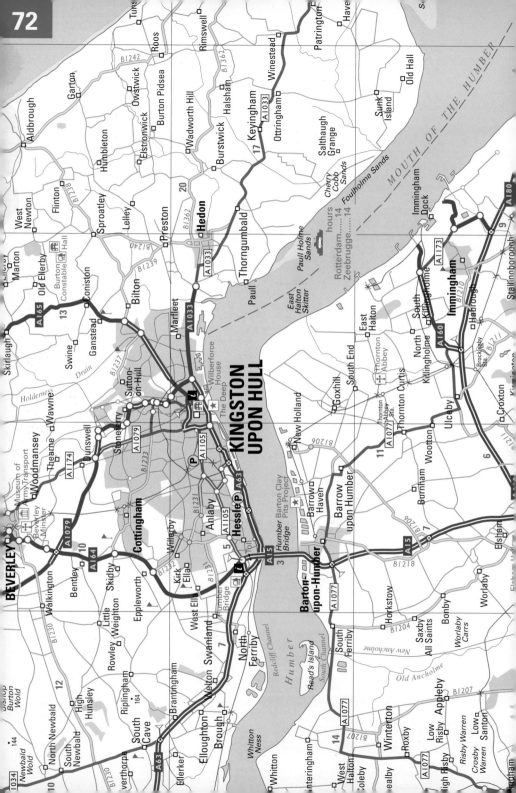

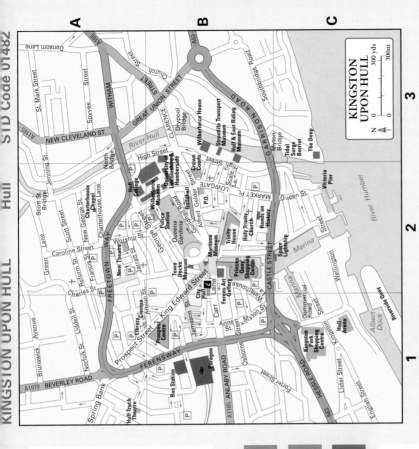

KINGSTON UPON HULL

N

0 · 300 yds
0 · 300m

INDEX TO STREET NAMES

Albion Street	B1	Garrison Road	B3	New George
Alfred Gelder	B2	George Street	B2	Street	A2
Street		Great Union	A3	Norfolk Street	A1
Anlaby Road	B1	Street		North Bridge	A2
Anne Street	B1	Green Lane	A2	Osborne Street	B1
Beverley Road	A1	Guildhall Road	B2	Porter Street	C1
Brunswick Avenue	A1	Hessle Road	C1	Prospect Street	A1
Caroline Street	A2	High Street	A3	Queen Street	C2
Carr Lane	B1	Jameson Street	B1	Reform Street	A2
Castle Street	B2	Jarratt Street	A2	St. Mark Street	A3
Charles Street	A2	Jenning Street	A2	Scale Lane	B2
Charterhouse	A2	King Edward	B1	Scott Street	A2
Lane		Street		Scott Street	A2
Church Street	B3	Kingston Street	C1	Bridge	
Clarence Street	B3	Liddell Street	A3	Southbridge Road	B3
Cleveland Street	A3	Lister Street	C1	Spring Bank	A1
Dansom Lane	A3	Lowgate	B2	Spyvee Street	A3
English Street	C1	Market Place	B2	Waterhouse Lane	B1
Ferensway	A1	Myton Street	B1	Wellington Street	C2
Francis Street	A2	New Cleveland	A1	Witham	A3
Freetown Way	A1	Street		Worship Street	A2

TOURIST INFORMATION ☎ 01482 223559
1 PARAGON STREET,
KINGSTON UPON HULL, HU1 3NA

HOSPITAL A & E ☎ 01482 328541
HULL ROYAL INFIRMARY, ANLABY ROAD,
KINGSTON UPON HULL, HU3 2JZ

COUNCIL OFFICE ☎ 01482 300300
GUILDHALL, ALFRED GELDER STREET,
KINGSTON UPON HULL, HU1 2AA

Kingston upon Hull (Commonly known as Hull.) *Hull* Population: 310,636. City, port at confluence of Rivers Humber and Hull, 50m/80km E of Leeds. Much of town destroyed during bombing of World War II; town centre has been rebuilt. Formerly had a thriving fishing industry. Major industry nowadays is frozen food processing. Restored docks, cobble streeted Old Town and modern marina. Universities. Birthplace of William Wilberforce, slavery abolitionist, 1759. Wilberforce Museum covers history of slavery. Streetlife Transport Museum. Town Docks Museum explores city's maritime history. Famous for associations with poets Andrew Marvell, Stevie Smith and Philip Larkin.

WEB-SITE | www.hullcc.gov.uk

LOCAL RADIO | BBC RADIO HUMBERSIDE 95.9 FM
MAGIC 1161 AM, VIKING FM 96.9 FM

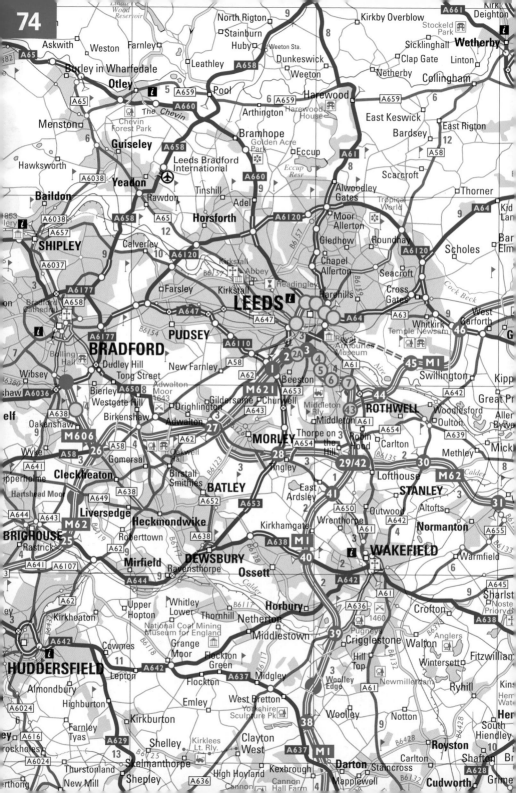

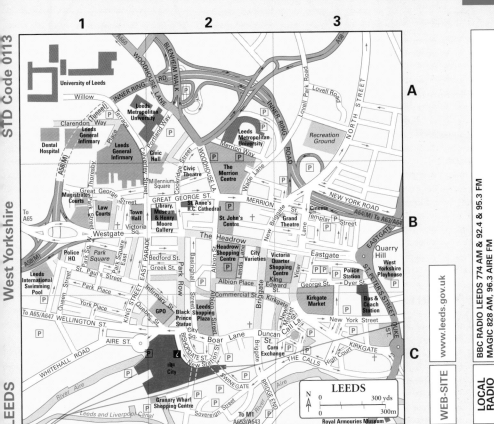

STD Code 0113

West Yorkshire

LEEDS

www.leeds.gov.uk

WEB-SITE

BBC RADIO LEEDS 774 AM & 92.4 & 95.3 FM
MAGIC 828 AM, 96.3 AIRE FM

LOCAL RADIO

LEEDS
N 0   300 yds
   0   300m
Royal Armouries Museum

INDEX TO STREET NAMES

TOURIST INFORMATION ☎ 0113 242 5242
GATEWAY YORKSHIRE, THE ARCADE,
CITY STATION, LEEDS, W. YORKSHIRE, LS1 1PL

HOSPITAL A & E ☎ 0113 243 2799
LEEDS GENERAL INFIRMARY,
GREAT GEORGE STREET, LEEDS, LS1 3EX

COUNCIL OFFICE ☎ 0113 234 8080
CIVIC HALL, CALVERLEY STREET,
LEEDS, LS1 1UR

Leeds *W. Yorks.* Population: 424,194. City, commercial and industrial city on River Aire and on Leeds and Liverpool Canal, 36m/58km NE of Manchester and 170m/274km NW of London. Previously important for textile industry. Prospered during Victorian period, the architecture of a series of ornate arcades containing some magnificent clocks reflecting the affluence of this time. City Art Gallery has a fine collection of 20c British Art. Edwardian Kirkgate Market is the largest in north of England. Royal Armouries Museum houses arms and armour collection from the Tower of London. Universities. Leeds Bradford International Airport at Yeadon, 7m/11km NW.

STD Code 0116

LEICESTER

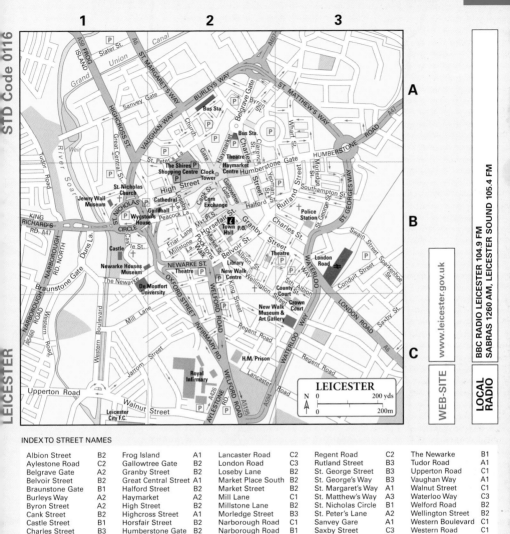

www.leicester.gov.uk

WEB-SITE

BBC RADIO LEICESTER 104.9 FM
SABRAS 1260 AM, LEICESTER SOUND 105.4 FM

LOCAL RADIO

INDEX TO STREET NAMES

The Newarke	B1
Tudor Road	A1
Upperton Road	C1
Vaughan Way	A1
Walnut Street	C1
Waterloo Way	C3
Welford Road	B2
Wellington Street	B2
Western Boulevard	C1
Western Road	C1
Wharf Street	A3
Yeoman Street	B2

TOURIST INFORMATION ☎ 0116 299 8888
7-9 EVERY STREET, TOWN HALL SQUARE,
LEICESTER, LE1 6AG

HOSPITAL A & E ☎ 0116 254 1414
LEICESTER ROYAL INFIRMARY,
INFIRMARY SQUARE, LEICESTER, LE1 5WW

COUNCIL OFFICE ☎ 0116 252 6480
COUNCIL OFFICES, NEW WALK CENTRE,
WELFORD PLACE, LEICESTER, LE1 6ZG

Leicester *Leic.* Population: 318,518. City, county town and commercial and industrial centre on River Soar, on site of Roman town of Ratae Coritanorum, 89m/143km NW of London. Industries include hosiery and footwear, alongside more modern industries. Universities. Many historic remains including Jewry Wall (English Heritage), one of largest surviving sections of Roman wall in the country, Roman baths and a medieval guildhall. Saxon Church of St. Nicholas. 11c St. Martin's Cathedral. Victorian clock tower. Newarke Houses Museum explores the city's social history. Home to England's second biggest street festival after Notting Hill Carnival. Joseph Merrick, the 'Elephant Man' born and lived here.

Gainsborough

Hall
undby
Bole
Wheatley
verton
thorpe
eswell
dbeck
east
ton
Darlton
Ragnal
3

Springthorpe
Heapham
Upton
Kexby
Lea
Khaith
Sturton
le Steeple
Littleborough
Marton
10
Gate
Burton
Willingham
Normanby
by Stow
Stow
A156
South
Leverton
Cottam
A1500
Sturton by Stow
Rampton
Brampton
Torksey
Stokeham
Laughterton
Fenton
Laneham
Kettlethorpe
Dunham
Toll
Newton on
Trent
Saxilby
A1133
Thorney
Broadholme
A57
Skellingthorpe

Harpswell
Glentworth
Fillingham
Coates
Ingham
Cammeringham
Brattleby
Thorpe
in the Fallows
Aisthorpe
Scampton
Bransby
Ingleby
Broxholme
North
Carlton
South
Carlton
Burton
70
B1398

Caenby
Corner
Normanby-by-
Spital
Caenby
Owmby-by-Spital
Tof
Saxby
Spridlington
11
Cold
Hanworth
Hackthorn
A15
Welton
Ryland
15
Dunholme
Snarford
Stainton by Lan
Scoth
Sudbrooke
A46
Nettleham
10
Reepham
Cherr
A158

Ermine Street
B1398

Roman Road
Till
B1241
B1190

1
Cath
LINCOLN
A57
Washingborough
i
B1308
Canwick
Heighing

North
Clifton
South
Clifton
A1133
Harby
Wigsley
Doddington
A46
Hartsholme
B1378
B1190
Boultham
Bracebridge
Bracebridge
Heath
Branston
B1188

12
Normanton
on Trent
Weston
Grassthorpe
Spalford
North
Scarle
Eagle
Whisby
Swallow
Beck
A607
Waddington
B1178

Sutton on
Trent
Girton
Besthorpe
South
Scarle
Thorpe on
the Hill
A1434
North
Hykeham
South
Hykeham
A15
A46

Carlton-on-Trent
A1133
Cromwell
Collingham
Swinderby
Haddington
Aubourn
Harmston
B1178

16
Fosse Way
Doddington
Hall
Aubourn
Hall
Thurlby
Coleby
B1202
Methe

A46
Holme
North
Muskham
Langford
Brough
Norton
Disney
Boothby Graffoe
Navenby
13

hley
le Carlton
Muskham
m
Winthorpe
Danethorpe
Hill
Stapleford
Carlton-le-
Moorland
Wellingore
A607
15
S

A616
2
A617
pe
Newark
A46
B6326
A1
i
A17
10
Coddington
Beckingham
A17
Brant
Broughton
Welbourn

**NEWARK-ON-
TRENT**
Hawton
Balderton
Barnby
in the
Willows
Sutton
Stragglethorpe
Leadenham
Temple Bruer
A15

Thorpe
toke
Claypole
Stubton
Fenton
Fulbeck
Hall
Fulbeck
A17
Cranwell
Leasingh
Witham
Brant
Langford
B6326
A607
B1429
Witham

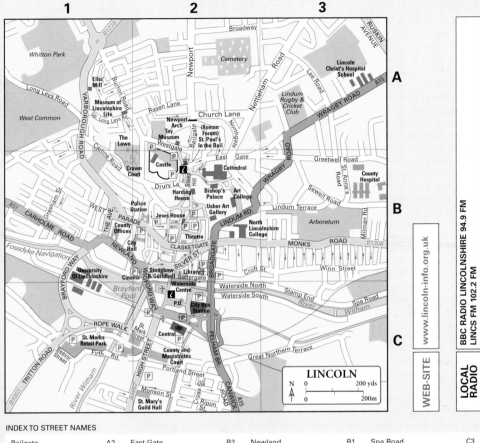

LINCOLN

N   0 _____ 200 yds
    0 _____ 200m

WEB-SITE www.lincoln-info.org.uk

LOCAL RADIO BBC RADIO LINCOLNSHIRE 94.9 FM / LINCS FM 102.2 FM

INDEX TO STREET NAMES

TOURIST INFORMATION ☎ 01522 873213
9 CASTLE HILL, LINCOLN,
LINCOLNSHIRE, LN1 3AA

HOSPITAL A & E ☎ 01522 512512
LINCOLN COUNTY HOSPITAL,
GREETWELL ROAD, LINCOLN, LN2 5QY

COUNCIL OFFICE ☎ 01522 552222
COUNTY OFFICES, NEWLAND,
LINCOLN, LN1 1YG

Lincoln *Lincs.* Population: 80,281. City, county town and cathedral city on River Witham, on site of Roman town of Lindum, 120m/193km N of London. City grew as a result of strategic importance in the wool trade. Many ancient monuments and archaeological features. Castle built by William I. 13c cathedral, is the third largest in Britain with its three towers on hilltop dominating the skyline. Carvings in the Angel Choir include the stone figure of the Lincoln Imp which is the city's emblem. Lincoln Bishop's Old Palace (English Heritage) is medieval building on S side of cathedral. 12c Jew's House. Museum of Lincolnshire Life. Universities.

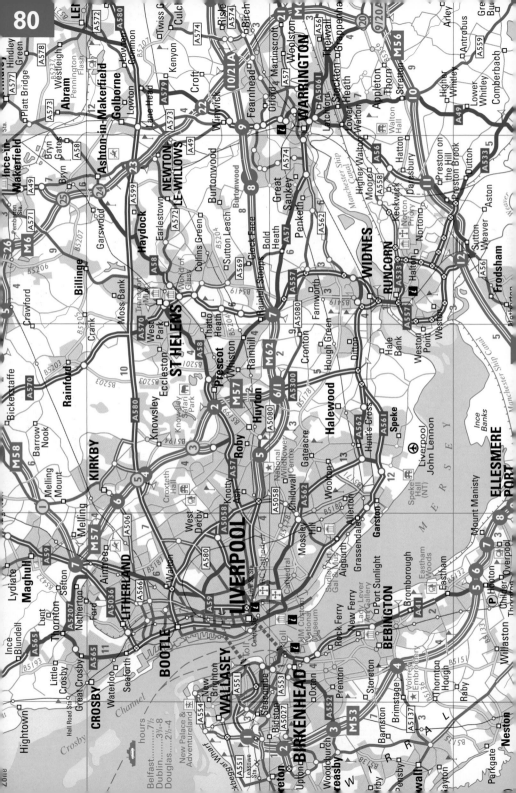

Merseyside   STD Code 0151

LIVERPOOL   Merseyside

INDEX TO STREET NAMES

Addison Street	A2	Gradwell Street	C2
Argyle Street	C2	Great Crosshall Street	A2
Bath Street	A1	Great Howard Street	A1
Berry Street	C3	Hanover Street	B2
Bold Street	C3	Hartley Quay	C1
Brownlow Hill	B3	Hatton Garden	B2
Brunswick Street	A3	Hawke Street	B3
Byrom Street	A2	Henry Street	B3
Canning Place	C2	Hood Street	B2
Castle Street	B2	Hunter Street	B2
Chapel Street	B1	James Street	B1
Cheapside	A2	King Edward Street	A1
Christian Street	A3	Leeds Street	A1
Church Street	B2	Lime Street	B3
Concert Street	C3	London Road	B3
Cook Street	B2	Lord Nelson Street	B3
Copperas Hill	B3	Lord Street	B2
Crosshall Street	B2	Marybone	A2
Dale Street	B2	Matthews Street	B2
Dawson Street	C2	Midghall Street	A2
Derby Square	B2	Moorfields	B2
Duke Street	C2	Mount Pleasant	C3
East Street	A1	Naylor Street	A1
Eaton Street	A1	New Quay	A1
Elliot Street	B3	North John Street	B2
Freemasons Row	A1	Old Hall Street	A1
Gascoyne Street	A1	Old Haymarket	B2
Gibraltar Row	A1	Paisley Street	A1
Gilbert Street	C2	Pall Mall	B1
Goree	A3		

Paradise Street	C2
Park Lane	C2
Parker Street	B3
Preston Street	B1
Princes Parade	A1
Queens Square	B2
Ranelagh Street	B3
Renshaw Street	B3
Roe Street	B3
Salthouse Quay	C1
School Lane	B2
Scotland Road	A2
Seel Street	C3
Sir Thomas Street	B2
Skelhorne Street	B3
Slater Street	C3
South John Street	B2
St. Anne Street	A3
St. John's Lane	B3
The Strand	B1
Tithebarn Street	A2
Vauxhall Road	A2
Victoria Street	B2
Wapping	C2
Water Street	B1
Waterloo Road	A1
Whitechapel	B2
William Brown Street	A3

TOURIST INFORMATION ☎ 09066 806886
MERSEYSIDE WELCOME CENTRE, CLAYTON SQ.
SHOPPING CEN, LIVERPOOL, MERSEYSIDE, L1 1QR

HOSPITAL A & E ☎ 0151 525 5980
UNIVERSITY HOSPITAL OF AINTREE, LOWER LANE,
FAZAKERLEY, LIVERPOOL, L9 7AL

COUNCIL OFFICE ☎ 0151 233 3000
MUNICIPAL BUILDINGS, DALE STREET,
LIVERPOOL, L69 2DH

Liverpool *Mersey.* Population: 481,786. City, major port and industrial city on River Mersey estuary, 178m/286km NW of London. Originally a fishing village it experienced rapid expansion during early 18c due to transatlantic trade in sugar, spice and tobacco and was involved in slave trade. Docks declined during 20c, now Albert Dock is home to shops, museums and Tate Liverpool. In 19c a multicultural city developed as Liverpool docks were point of departure for Europeans emigrating to America and Australia. Also became home to refugees from Irish potato famine of 1845. Present day Liverpool is home to variety of industries and many museums and art galleries. Also home of the Beatles, who performed at Liverpool's Cavern Club. Universities. Modern Anglican and Roman Catholic cathedrals. On Pier Head the famous Royal Liver Building is situated, topped by Liver Birds. Railway tunnel and two road tunnels under River Mersey to Wirral peninsula. Airport at Speke, 6m/10km.

WEB-SITE www.liverpool.gov.uk

LOCAL RADIO BBC RADIO MERSEYSIDE 95.8 FM
MAGIC 1548 AM, RADIO CITY 96.7 FM, JUICE 107.6 FM

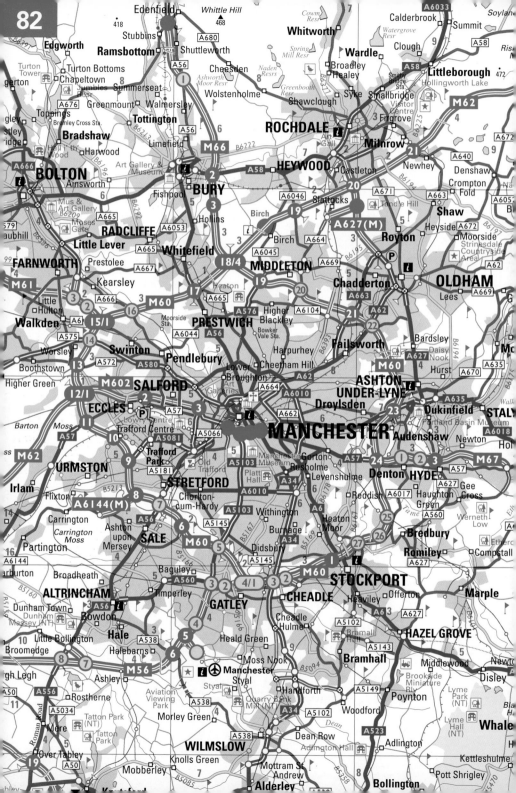

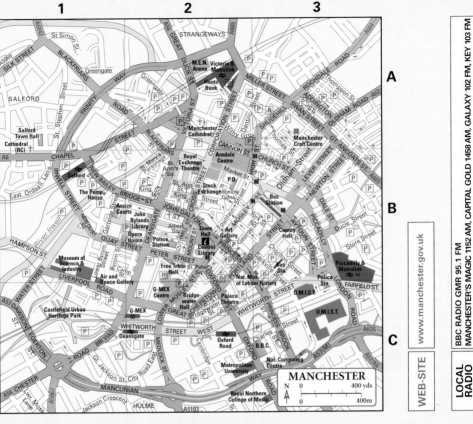

WEB-SITE www.manchester.gov.uk

LOCAL RADIO BBC RADIO GMR 95.1 FM · MANCHESTER'S MAGIC 1152 AM, CAPITAL GOLD 1458 AM, GALAXY 102 FM, KEY 103 FM

INDEX TO STREET NAMES

TOURIST INFORMATION ☎ 0161 234 3157/8
MANCHESTER VISITOR CENTRE, TOWN HALL
EXTENSION, LLOYD ST, MANCHESTER, M60 2LA

HOSPITAL A & E ☎ 0161 276 1234
MANCHESTER ROYAL INFIRMARY,
OXFORD ROAD, MANCHESTER, M13 9WL

COUNCIL OFFICE ☎ 0161 234 5000
TOWN HALL, ALBERT SQUARE,
MANCHESTER, M60 2LA

Manchester *Gt.Man.* Population: 402,889. City, important industrial, business, cultural and commercial centre and port, 164m/264km NW of London. Access for ships by River Mersey and Manchester Ship Canal, opened in 1894. 15c cathedral, formerly parish church, has widest nave in England. Experienced rapid growth during industrial revolution. In 1750, Manchester was essentially still a village. During Victorian era, city was global cotton milling capital. Present day city is home to wide range of industries and is unofficial capital of nation's 'youth culture'. Major shopping centres include Arndale and Trafford Centres. Universities. International airport 9m/14km S of city centre.

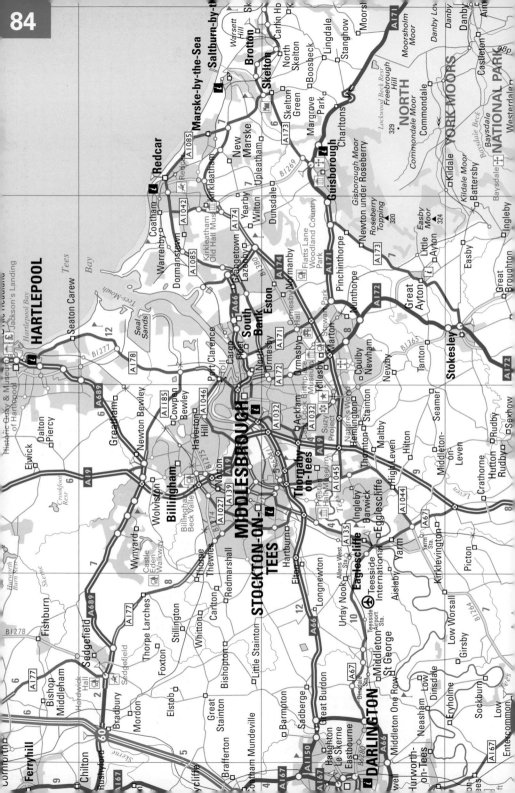

MIDDLESBROUGH

STD Code 01642

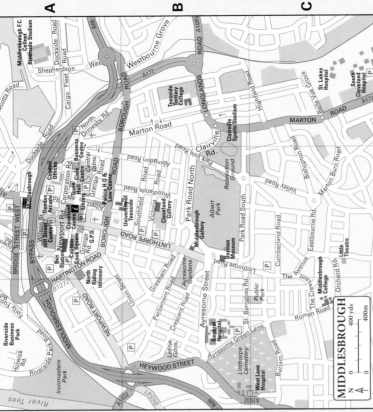

MIDDLESBROUGH

N

| 0 | 400 yds |
| 0 | 400m |

INDEX TO STREET NAMES

Abingdon Road	B2	Marton Burn Road	C2
Albert Road	A2	Marton Road	B3/C3
Ayresome Green Lane	B1	Newport Road	A1/A2
Ayresome Street	B1	North Ormesby Road	A3
Belle Vue Grove	C3	Orchard Road	C1
Bishopton Road	C2	Park Road North	B2
Borough Road	A2/C3	Park Road South	B2
Bridge Street West	A2	Park Vale Road	B2
Burlam Road	C1	Parliament Road	B1
Cargo Fleet Road	A3	Riverside Park Road	A1
Clairville Road	B2	Roman Road	C1
Corporation Road	A2	St. Barnabas Road	B1
Crescent Road	B1	Scotts Road	A3
Cumberland Road	C2	Sheperdson Way	A3
Dockside Road	A2/A3	Snowdon Road	A2
Eastbourne Road	C2	Southfield Road	B2
Forty Foot Road	A1	The Avenue	C2
Grange Road	A2	The Crescent	C1
Gresham Road	B1	Union Street	B1
Hartington Road	A1	Valley Road	C2
Heywood Street	B1	Victoria Road	B2
Highfield Road	C3	Westbourne Grove	B3
Holwick Road	A1	Wilson Street	A2
Linthorpe Road	C2	Woodlands Road	B2
Longlands Road	B3		

TOURIST INFORMATION ☎ 01642 358086/243425
99-101 ALBERT ROAD,
MIDDLESBROUGH, TS1 2PA

HOSPITAL A & E ☎ 01642 617617
NORTH TEES GENERAL HOSPITAL, HARDWICK ROAD,
STOCKTON-ON-TEES, TS19 8PE

COUNCIL OFFICE ☎ 01642 245432
MUNICIPAL BUILDINGS, PO BOX 99A,
RUSSELL STREET, MIDDLESBROUGH, TS1 2QQ

WEB-SITE www.middlesbrough.gov.uk

LOCAL RADIO BBC RADIO CLEVELAND 95 FM
MAGIC 1170 AM, TFM 96.6 FM, CENTURY FM 100.7 FM

Middlesbrough *Middbro*. Population: 147,430. Town, port, with extensive dock area, on S bank of River Tees, forming part of Teesside urban complex. A former iron and steel town, its chief industries now involve oil and petrochemicals. Unusual 1911 transporter bridge over River Tees. University of Teesside. Captian Cook Birthplace Museum in Stewart Park at Marton.

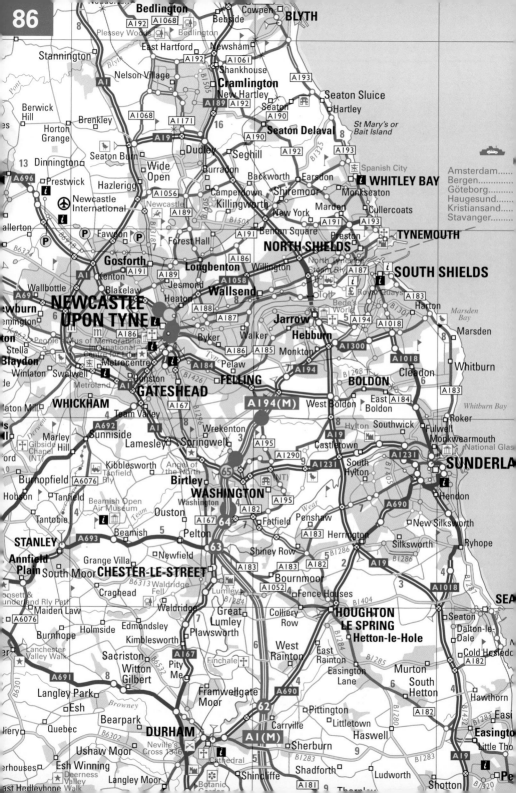

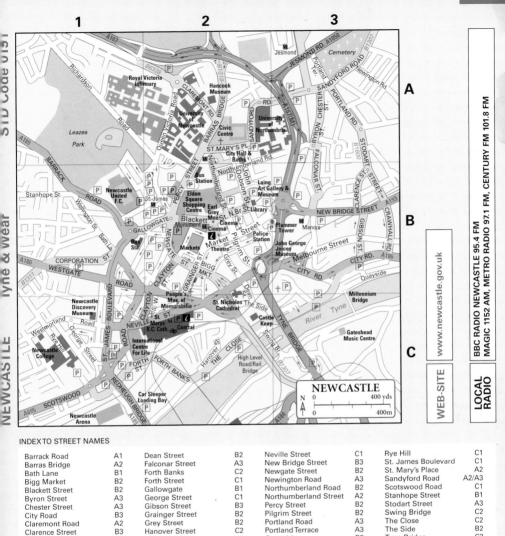

NEWCASTLE

N 0 — 400 yds
0 — 400m

INDEX TO STREET NAMES

TOURIST INFORMATION ☎ 0191 277 8000
128 GRAINGER STREET, NEWCASTLE
UPON TYNE, TYNE & WEAR, NE1 5AF

HOSPITAL A & E ☎ 0191 273 8811
NEWCASTLE GENERAL HOSPITAL, WESTGATE
ROAD, NEWCASTLE UPON TYNE, NE64 6BE

COUNCIL OFFICE ☎ 0191 232 8520
CIVIC CENTRE, BARRAS BRIDGE,
NEWCASTLE UPON TYNE, NE99 1RD

Newcastle upon Tyne T. & W. Population: 189,150. City, port on River Tyne about 11m/17km upstream from river mouth and 80m/129km N of Leeds. The 'new castle' of city's name started in 1080 by Robert Curthose, eldest son of William the Conqueror. 13c castle gatehouse known as 'Black Gate'. Commercial and industrial centre, previously dependent upon coalmining and shipbuilding. In its heyday, 25 percent of world's shipping built here. Cathedral dates from 14 to 15c. Bessie Surtees House (English Heritage) comprises 16c and 17c merchants' houses. Tyne Bridge, opened in 1928 and longest of its type at time. Venerable Bede (AD 672-735) born near Jarrow. Catherine Cookson, writer, also born in Jarrow. Universities. Newcastle International Airport 5m/8km NW.

WEB-SITE — www.newcastle.gov.uk

LOCAL RADIO — BBC RADIO NEWCASTLE 95.4 FM, MAGIC 1152 AM, METRO RADIO 97.1 FM, CENTURY FM 101.8 FM

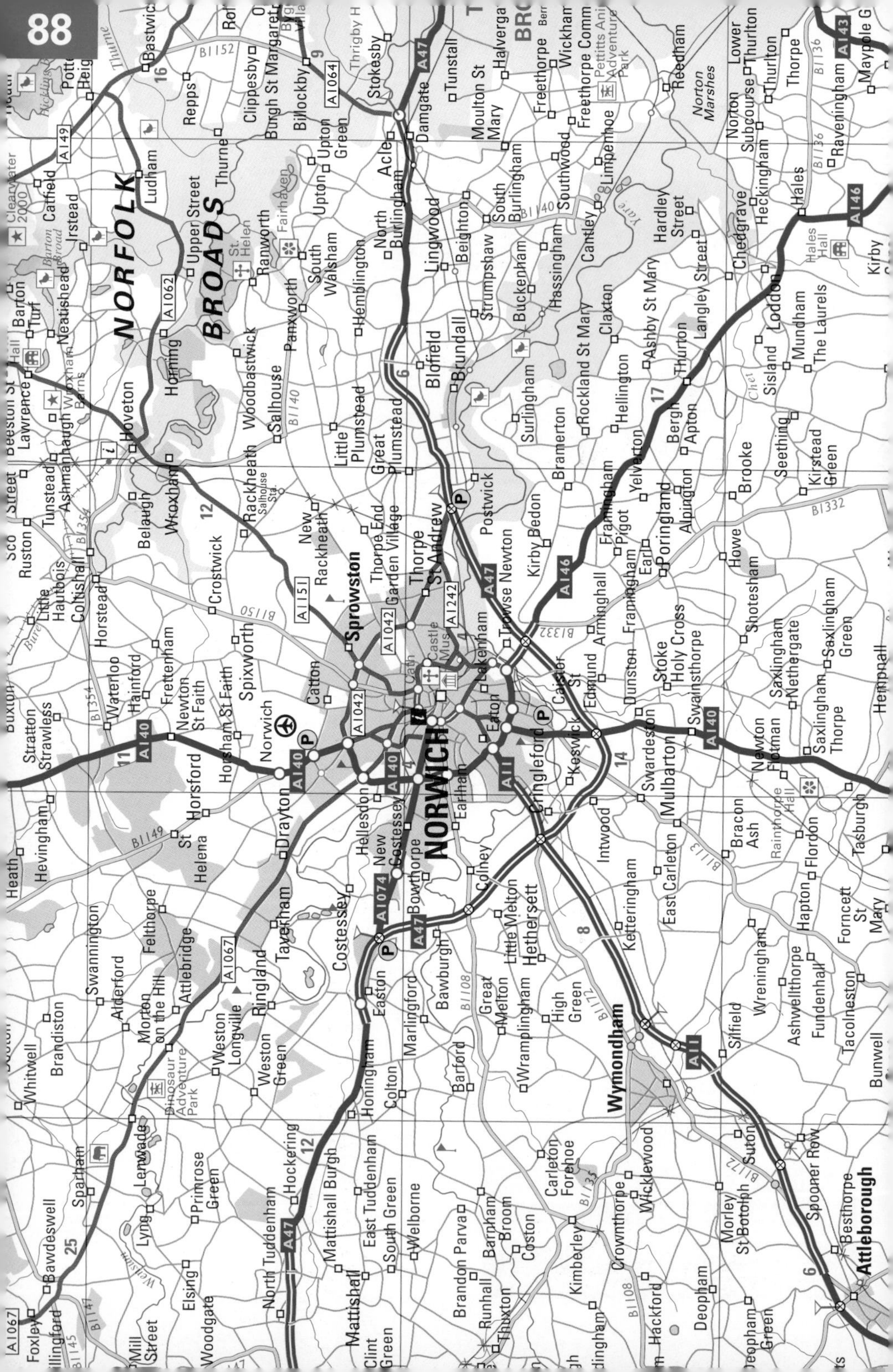

NORFOLK
BROADS
NORWICH
Sprowston
Wymondham
Attleborough
Hoveton
Wroxham
Horning
Ludham
Potter Heigham
Bastwick
Repps
Thurne
Clippesby
Burgh St Margaret
Billockby
Stokesby
Acle
Upton
Upton Green
Ranworth
South Walsham
Panxworth
Woodbastwick
Salhouse
Upper Street
Catfield
Irstead
Neatishead
Barton Turf
Beeston St Lawrence
Ashmanhaugh
Tunstead
Sco Ruston
Coltishall
Little Hautbois
Horstead
Belaugh
Rackheath
New Rackheath
Crostwick
Spixworth
Frettenham
Hainford
Waterloo
Stratton Strawless
Newton St Faith
Horsham St Faith
Horsford
Hevingham
St Helena
Drayton
Taverham
Costessey
New Costessey
Hellesdon
Catton
Thorpe End Garden Village
Thorpe St Andrew
Great Plumstead
Little Plumstead
Hemblington
North Burlingham
South Burlingham
Lingwood
Blofield
Brundall
Beighton
Strumpshaw
Buckenham
Hassingham
Cantley
Limpenhoe
Southwood
Freethorpe
Freethorpe Common
Wickhampton
Halvergate
Tunstall
Moulton St Mary
Damgate
Reedham
Norton Marshes
Thurlton
Norton Subcourse
Heckingham
Hales
Hales Hall
Kirby Cane
Raveningham
Thorpe
Maypole Green
Chedgrave
Loddon
Hardley Street
Langley Street
Claxton
Ashby St Mary
Rockland St Mary
Hellington
Surlingham
Bramerton
Postwick
Kirby Bedon
Trowse Newton
Lakenham
Eaton
Earlham
Cringleford
Keswick
Caistor St Edmund
Arminghall
Framingham Pigot
Framingham Earl
Poringland
Yelverton
Alpington
Thurton
Bergh Apton
Stoke Holy Cross
Dunston
Swardeston
Swainsthorpe
Mulbarton
East Carleton
Ketteringham
Intwood
Hethersett
Little Melton
Great Melton
Colney
Bawburgh
Bowthorpe
Easton
Marlingford
Honingham
Colton
Barford
Wramplingham
High Green
Bracon Ash
Newton Flotman
Saxlingham Thorpe
Saxlingham Nethergate
Saxlingham Green
Shotesham
Howe
Brooke
Seething
Kirstead Green
Mundham
Sisland
The Laurels
Hempnall
Tasburgh
Flordon
Rainthorpe Hall
Hapton
Forncett St Mary
Tacolneston
Fundenhall
Ashwellthorpe
Wreningham
Silfield
Bunwell
Spooner Row
Suton
Besthorpe
Morley St Botolph
Deopham
Deopham Green
Wicklewood
Crownthorpe
Carleton Forehoe
Kimberley
Hackford
Coston
Barnham Broom
Brandon Parva
Runhall
Thuxton
Welborne
East Tuddenham
South Green
Mattishall Burgh
Mattishall
Clint Green
North Tuddenham
Hockering
Elsing
Woodgate
Primrose Green
Lyng
Lenwade
Sparham
Bawdeswell
Foxley
Mill Street
Weston Longville
Weston Green
Ringland
Attlebridge
Morton on the Hill
Alderford
Swannington
Felthorpe
Brandiston
Whitwell
Dinosaur Adventure Park
Pettitts Animal Adventure Park
Fairhaven
St Helen
Wroxham Barns
Clearwater 2000
Castle Mus
Cath
Thrigby Hall
A47
A140
A146
A11
A1074
A1042
A1242
A1151
A1062
A1067
A143
A149
A1064
B1140
B1152
B1354
B1150
B1149
B1332
B1108
B1172
B1135
B1113
B1136
B1145
Bure
Yare
Chet
Wensum
Thurne

Map of Norwich

NORWICH
N   0   400 yds
    0   400m

INDEX TO STREET NAMES

Albion Way	C3	Grapes Hill	C1
All Saints Green	C2	Grove Road	B2
Bakers Road	A1	Grove Walk	C1
Bank Plain	B2	Gurney Road	A1
Barker Street	A1	Hall Road	C3
Barn Road	B1	Heigham Street	A1
Barrack Street	A2	Ipswich Road	C3
Bedford Street	B2	Ketts Hill	A2
Ber Street	C2	King Street	B3
Bethel Street	B1	Koblenz Avenue	C3
Bishopbridge Road	B3	Lower Clarence Road	C2
Bishopgate	B3	Magdalen Street	A2
Brazen Gate	C2	Magpie Road	A1
Brunswick Road	C1	Market Avenue	B2
Bullclose Road	A2	Mountergate	B2
Carrow Road	C3	Mousehold Street	A1
Chapel Field Road	B1	Newmarket Road	C1
Chapelfield North	B1	Newmarket Street	C1
City Road	C2	Oak Street	A1
Clarence Road	C3	Orchard Street	B1
Colegate	A2	Palace Street	B2
Coslany Street	B1	Pitt Street	A1
Cowgate	A2	Prince of Wales Road	B2
Dereham Road	B1	Pottergate	B1
Duke Street	B1	Queens Road	C2
Earlham Road	A1	Rampant Horse Street	B2
Edward Street	A2	Riverside	C3
Elm Hill	B2	Riverside Road	B3
Fishergate	A2	Rosary Road	B3
		Rose Lane	B2
		Rouen Road	C2
Rupert Street	C1	St. Martin's Road	A1
St. Andrew's Street	B2	St. Stephen's Road	C1
St. Augustine's Street	A1	St. Stephen's Street	C1
St. Benedict's Street	B1	Silver Road	A2
St. Crispin's Road	A2	Southwell Road	C2
St. George's Street	A2	Surrey Street	C1
St. Giles Street	B1	Sussex Street	A1
St. Leonards Road	B3	Theatre Street	B1
St. Martin's Road	A1	Thorn Lane	C2
St. Stephen's Street	C1	Thorpe Road	B3
		Tombland	B2
		Trinity Street	C1
		Union Street	C1
		Unthank Road	C1
		Vauxhall Street	A2
		Victoria Street	B1
		Wensum Street	B2
		Wessex Street	C1
		Westwick Street	B1
		Wherry Road	C3
		Whitefriars	A2

TOURIST INFORMATION ☎ 01603 666071
THE FORUM, MILLENNIUM PLAIN,
NORWICH, NR2 1TF

HOSPITAL A & E ☎ 01603 286286
NORFOLK & NORWICH HOSPITAL,
BRUNSWICK ROAD, NORWICH, NR1 3SR

COUNCIL OFFICE ☎ 01603 622233
CITY HALL, ST. PETER'S STREET,
NORWICH, NR2 1NH

WEB-SITE   www.norwich.gov.uk

LOCAL RADIO   BBC RADIO NORFOLK 95.1 & 104.4 FM
CLASSIC GOLD AMBER 1152 AM, BROADLAND 102 102.4 FM

Norwich *Norf.* Population: 171,304. City, county town and cathedral city at confluence of River Wensum and River Yare, 98m/158km NE of London. Middle ages saw Norwich become second richest city in country through exporting textiles. Medieval streets and buildings are well preserved. Sections of 14c flint city wall defences still exist, including Cow Tower (English Heritage). Current chief industries are high technology and computer based. Notable buildings include partly Norman cathedral with second highest spire in Britain, Norman castle with keep (now museum and art gallery), 15c guildhall, modern city hall, numerous medieval churches. University of East Anglia 2m/4km W of city centre. Airport 3m/5km N.

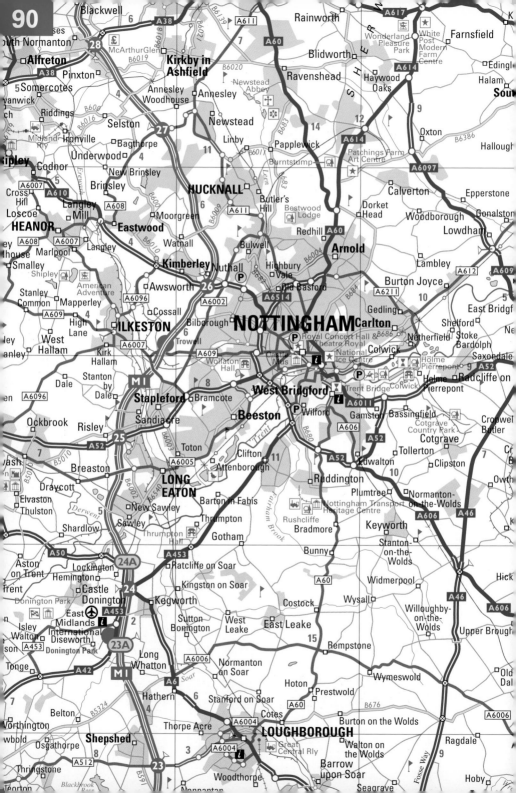

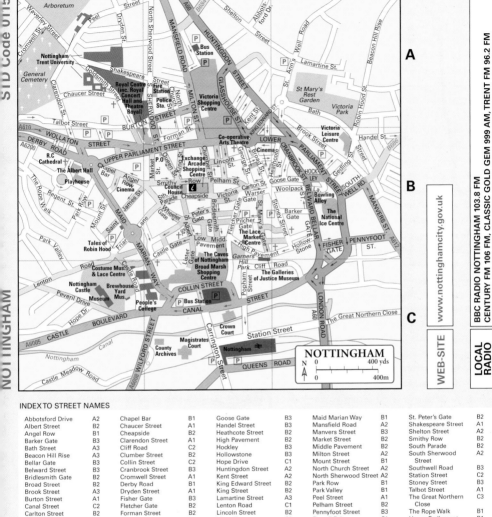

STD Code 0115

NOTTINGHAM

WEB-SITE www.nottinghamcity.gov.uk

LOCAL RADIO
BBC RADIO NOTTINGHAM 103.8 FM
CENTURY FM 106 FM, CLASSIC GOLD GEM 999 AM, TRENT FM 96.2 FM

INDEX TO STREET NAMES

TOURIST INFORMATION ☎ 0115 915 5330
1-4 SMITHY ROW,
NOTTINGHAM, NG1 2BY

HOSPITAL A & E ☎ 0115 924 9924
QUEENS MEDICAL CENTRE, UNIVERSITY HOSP,
DERBY ROAD, NOTTINGHAM, NG7 2UH

COUNCIL OFFICE ☎ 0115 915 5555
THE GUILDHALL, SOUTH SHERWOOD STREET,
NOTTINGHAM, NG1 4BT

Nottingham *Nott.* Population: 270,222. City, on River Trent, 45m/72km NE of Birmingham. Originally Saxon town built on one of a pair of hills. In 1068, Normans built castle on other hill and both communities traded in valley between. Important commercial, industrial, entertainment and sports centre. Key industries include manufacture of lace, mechanical products, tobacco and pharmaceuticals. 17c castle, restored 19c, houses museum and art gallery. Two universities. Repertory theatre.

6

Marsh Gibbon • Edgcott • Grendon Underwood • Kingswood • Ludgershall • Wotton Underwood • Ashendon • Dorton • Chilton • Easington • Long Crendon • Shabbington • Thame • Moreton • Sydenham • Postcombe • Lewknor • Pyrton • Adwell • Tetsworth

A41 • A4129 • A4010 • B4011 • A329 • A418 • A40 • M40 • B4012 • A4074

Launton • Blackthorn • Piddington • Upper Arncott • Murcott • Oddington • Boarstall • Oakley • Worminghall • Ickford • Waterperry • Waterstock • Tiddington • Rycote Chapel • Great Haseley • Little Haseley • Stoke Talmage • Chalgrove

Bicester • Chesterton • Ambrosden • Wendlebury • Merton • Fencott • Charlton-on-Otmoor • Horton-cum-Studley • Stanton St John • Forest Hill • Holton • Wheatley • Horspath • Cuddesdon • Denton • Chislehampton • Stadhampton • Chalgrove

M40 • A34 • B430 • B4027 • A4095 • A4260

Middleton Stoney • Kirtlington • Weston-on-the-Green • Bletchingdon • Islip • Noke • Woodeaton • Water Eaton • Elsfield • Marston • Headington • Shotover • Cowley • Garsington • Toot Baldon • Marsh Baldon • Nuneham Courtenay

Northbrook • Nethercott • Tackley • Shipton-on-Cherwell • Thrupp • Hampton Gay • Kidlington • Begbroke • Sunnymead • Summertown • OXFORD • Iffley • Littlemore • Sandford-on-Thames • Radley • Abingdon

Kiddington • Rousham Gap • Glympton • Wootton • Woodstock • Bladon • Yarnton • Cassington • Botley • North Hinksey • South Hinksey • Kennington • Sandleigh • Wootton • Sunningwell • Shippon

Kidlington • Blenheim Palace • Long Hanborough • Church Hanborough • Eynsham • Swinford • Wolvercote • Wytham • Cumnor • Bessels Leigh • Dry Sandford • Cothill • Garford • Marcham

Charlbury • Fawler • Finstock • Ramsden • Combe • East End • New Yatt • North Leigh • Freeland • Barnard Gate • South Leigh • Stanton Harcourt • Northmoor • Appleton • Netherton • Fyfield • Frilford • Kingston Bagpuize

Fulwell • Over Kiddington • Ditchley • Stonesfield • Hailey • Crawley • High Cogges • Ducklington • Brighthampton • Yelford • Standlake • Shifford • Newbridge • Longworth • Hinton Waldrist • Pusey

Witney • Aston • Cote • Chimney • Buckland • Carswell Marsh

Eastend • Spelsbury • Leafield • Minster Lovell • Curbridge

Evenlode • Windrush • Thames

Oxfordshire   STD Code 01865   OXFORD

A map of Oxford showing streets, colleges, and landmarks including River Cherwell, University Parks, Magdalen, Botanic Garden, St Catherine's, St Hilda's, Christ Church Meadow, Iffley Rd. A4158, Magdalen Br., Longwall St., New College, Merton, Mansfield Rd., University Museum of Natural History, Pitt Rivers Museum, Linacre College, St. Cross Road, University Science Area, Manchester, Holywell St., Queen's, All Souls, Radcliffe Camera, Bodleian Library, Sheldonian Theatre, Wadham, Rhodes House, Keble, Parks Road, Engineering Laboratory, Radcliffe Science Library, St. John's, Trinity, Balliol, Broad St., History of Science Mus., Exeter, Brasenose, Lincoln, Town Hall, Christ Church, Cathedral, Bate Collection, Police Station, Salter Bros. Boat Trips, St. Aldate's, Folly Br. A4144, Corpus Christi, Oriel, Merton, HIGH STREET, Mus. of Oxford, Market, Turl St., Cornmarket, St. Giles, Banbury Road, St. Anne's, St. Antony's, Woodstock Road, Observatory, Radcliffe Infirmary, Somerville, Walton Street, Ruskin, Worcester, Regents Park, Ashmolean Museum, Theatres, Beaumont St., St. Peter's, Clarendon Shopping Centre, Bus Sta., George St., Nuffield, St. Ebbe's, Mus. of Modern Art, Westgate Shopping Centre, Castle, County Hall, New Road, Pembroke, Littlegate St., Council Offices, Oxford College of Further Education, Hollybush Row, Botley Road, Hythe Br. St., Park End St., Oxpens Road, Ice Rink, Oxford Canal, Cricket Ground, Nelson St., Jericho, Albert Street, Juxon St., Plantation Rd., St. Bernards Rd., River Thames or Isis

OXFORD

N
400 yds
400m

A B C   1 2 3

TOURIST INFORMATION ☎ 01865 726871
15-16 BROAD STREET,
OXFORD, OX1 3AS

HOSPITAL A & E ☎ 01865 741166
JOHN RADCLIFFE HOSPITAL, HEADLEY WAY, HEADINGTON,
OXFORD, OX3 9DU

COUNCIL OFFICE ☎ 01865 249811
PO BOX 10,
OXFORD, OX1 1EN

Oxford *Oxon.* Population: 118,795. City, at confluence of Rivers Thames and Cherwell, 52m/84km NW of London. Began as Saxon settlement, flourished under Normans when it was chosen as royal residence. University dating from 13c, recognised as being among best in the world. Many notable buildings create spectacular skyline. Cathedral. Bodleian Library, second largest in UK. Ashmolean museum, oldest public museum in country. Tourist and commercial centre. Ancient St. Giles Fair held every September. Oxford Brookes University at Headington, 2m/4km E of city centre. Airport at Kidlington.

WEB-SITE www.oxford.gov.uk

LOCAL RADIO BBC RADIO OXFORD 95.2 FM
FOX FM 102.6 FM, FUSION 107.9 FM

PLYMOUTH

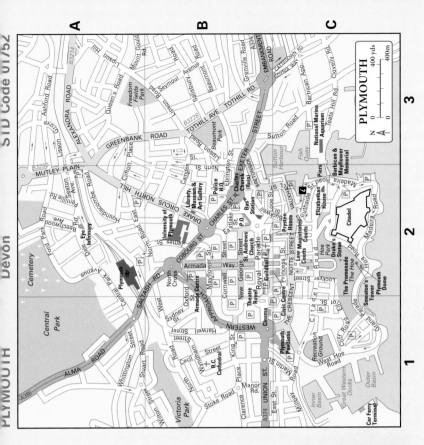

PLYMOUTH
N
0 .... 400 yds
0 .... 400m

WEB-SITE www.plymouth.gov.uk

LOCAL RADIO BBC RADIO DEVON 103.4 FM
CLASSIC GOLD 1152 AM, PLYMOUTH SOUND 97 FM

INDEX TO STREET NAMES

Alexandra Road	A3	Embankment		
Alma Road	A1	Road	B3	North Hill	B2
Armada Way	B2	Exeter Street	B2	North Road East	B2
Ashford Road	A3	Ford Park Road	A2	North Road West	B1
Barbican	C3	Gdynia Way	C3	North Street	C2
Beaumont Road	B3	Grand Parade	C1	Notte Street	C2
Beechwood		Greenbank Road	A3	Oxford Street	B1
Avenue	A2	Grenville Road	B3	Pentillie Road	A2
Bretonside	B2	Harwell Street	B1	Princess Street	C2
Buckwell Street	C2	Hoe Road	C2	Queen's Road	A3
Camden Street	B2	Houndiscombe		Royal Parade	B2
Cattledown Road	C3	Road	A2	Salisbury Road	B3
Cecil Street	B1	James Street	B2	Saltash Road	A1
Central Park		King Street	B1	Seaton Avenue	A2
Avenue	A1	Lipson Hill	C1	Seymour Avenue	B3
Charles Street	B2	Lipson Road	B3	Southside Street	C2
Citadel Road	C1	Lisson Grove	A3	Stoke Road	B1
Clarence Place	B1	Lockyer Street	C2	Stuart Road	A1
Cliff Road	C1	Looe Street	B2	Sutton Road	B3
Clifton Place	A2	Madeira Road	C1	Sydney Street	B1
Clovelly Road	C3	Manor Road	B1	Teats Hill Road	C3
Cobourg Street	B2	Martin Street	B1	The Crescent	C1
Cornwall Street	B2	Mayflower Street	B2	Tothill Avenue	B3
Dale Road	A2	Millbay Road	B1	Tothill Road	B3
Drake Circus	B2	Mount Gould	A3	Union Street	B1
East Street	C1	Mutley Plain	A2	Vauxhall Street	C1
Eastlake Street	B2	New George		West Hoe Road	C1
Ebrington Street	B2	Street	B2	Western Approach	A2
Elliot Street	C1	North Cross	B2	Whittington Street	B1
				Wilton Street	B1
				Wyndham Street	B2

TOURIST INFORMATION ☎ 01752 264849
ISLAND HOUSE, 9 THE BARBICAN,
PLYMOUTH, DEVON, PL1 2LS

HOSPITAL A & E ☎ 01752 777111
DERRIFORD HOSPITAL, DERRIFORD ROAD,
CROWNHILL, PLYMOUTH, PL6 8DH

COUNCIL OFFICE ☎ 01752 668000
CIVIC CENTRE, ARMADA WAY,
PLYMOUTH, PL1 2EW

Plymouth *Plym.* Population: 245,295. City, largest city in SW England, 100m/160km SW of Bristol. Port and naval base. Regional shopping centre. City centre rebuilt after bombing in World War II. Has strong commercial and naval tradition. In 1588 Sir Francis Drake sailed from Plymouth to defeat Spanish Armada. Captain Cook's voyages to Australia, South Seas and Antarctica all departed from here. University. Plymouth City Airport to N of city.

PORTSMOUTH

STD Code 023

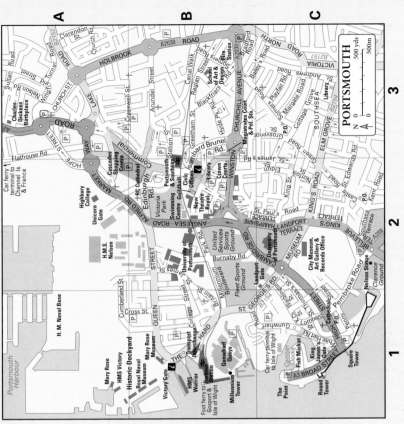

INDEX TO STREET NAMES

Alfred Road	B2	Green Road	C2
Anglesea Road	B2	Greetham Street	B3
Arundel Street	B3	Grosvenor Street	C3
Bailey's Road	C3	Gunwharf Road	C2
Bellevue Terrace	C2	Hampshire Terrace	C2
Blackfriars Road	B3	High Street	C3
Bradford Road	B3	Holbrook Road	A3
Britain Street	B1	Hope Street	A2
Broad Street	C1	Hyde Park Road	B3
Burnaby Road	B2	Isambard Brunel	B2
Cambridge Road	C2	Road	
Canal Walk	B3	Kent Road	C2
Castle Road	C2	King Charles Street	C1
Church Road	A3	King's Road	C2
Church Street	A3	King's Terrace	C2
Clarendon Street	A3	King Street	C2
College Street	B1	Lake Road	A3
Commercial Road	B2	Landport Terrace	C2
Cottage Grove	C3	Lombard Street	C1
Crasswell Street	A3	Margate Road	C3
Cross Street	A1	Market Way	A2
Cumberland Street	B1	Millennium	B1
Edinburgh Road	B2	Boulevard	
Eldon Street	C2	Museum Road	C2
Elm Grove	C3	Nelson Road	A3
Flathouse Road	A3	Norfolk Street	B2
Park Road	B2	St. Thomas's Street	C1
Pembroke Road	C1	Somers Road	B3
Penny Street	C1	Southsea Terrace	C2
Playfair Road	C3	Station Street	B3
Queen Street	B1	Sultan Road	A3
Raglan Street	B3	The Hard	C2
St. Andrews Road	C3	Turner Road	A3
St. Edward's Road	C2	Victoria Road North	C3
St. George's Road	B1	Warbington Street	C1
St. James Road	C2	White Hart Road	A2
St. James Street	C2	Wingfield Street	B1
St. Paul's Road	C2	Winston Churchill	
St. Thomas's Street	C1	Avenue	B2

TOURIST INFORMATION ☎ 023 9282 6722
THE HARD,
PORTSMOUTH, PO1 3QJ

HOSPITAL A & E ☎ 023 9228 6000
QUEEN ALEXANDRA HOSPITAL, SOUTHWICK
HILL ROAD, COSHAM, PORTSMOUTH, PO6 3LY

COUNCIL OFFICE ☎ 023 9282 2251
CIVIC OFFICES, GUILDHALL SQUARE,
PORTSMOUTH, PO1 2BG

Portsmouth *Ports.* Population: 174,690. City, port and naval base (Portsmouth Harbour, on W side of city) 65m/105km SW of London, extending from S end of Portsea Island to S slopes of Ports Down. Various industries, including tourism, financial services and manufacturing. Partly bombed in World War II and now rebuilt; however, some 18c buildings remain. Boat and hovercraft ferries to Isle of Wight. University. Two cathedrals. Nelson's ship, HMS Victory, in harbour, alongside which are remains of Henry VIII's flagship, Mary Rose, which sank in 1545. King James's Gate and Landport Gate were part of 17c defences, and Fort Cumberland is 18c coastal defence at Eastney (all English Heritage). Royal Garrison Church (English Heritage) was 16c chapel prior to Dissolution. Museums, many with nautical theme. City airport at N end of Portsea Island.

WEB-SITE www.portsmouth.gov.uk

LOCAL RADIO
BBC RADIO SOLENT 96.1 FM
CAPITAL GOLD 1170 AM, OCEAN FM 97.5 FM, THE QUAY 107.4 FM, WAVE 105.2 FM

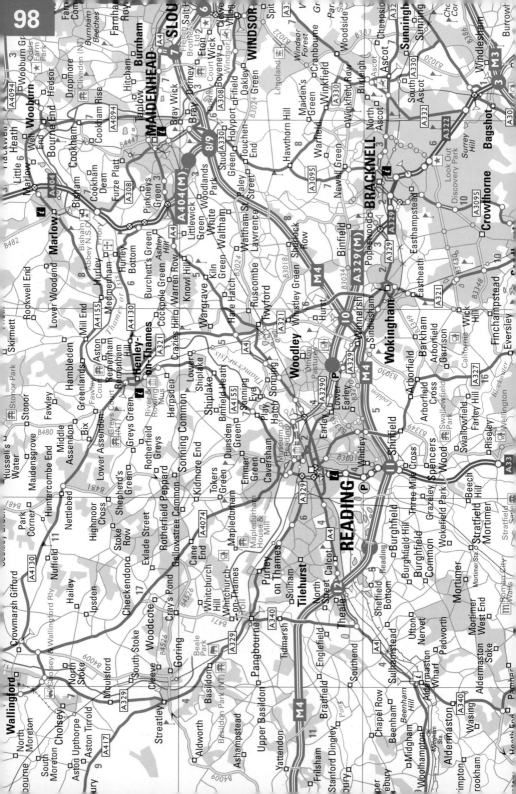

READING

STD Code 0118

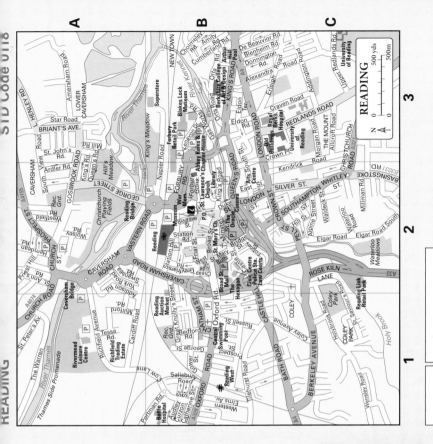

INDEX TO STREET NAMES

TOURIST INFORMATION ☎ 0118 956 6226
TOWN HALL, BLAGRAVE STREET,
READING, RG1 1QH

HOSPITAL A & E ☎ 0118 987 5111
ROYAL BERKSHIRE HOSPITAL, LONDON ROAD,
READING, RG1 5AN

COUNCIL OFFICE ☎ 0118 939 0900
CIVIC CENTRE, CIVIC OFFICES, (OFF CASTLE ST.)
READING, RG1 7TD

Reading *Read.* Town, county and industrial town and railway centre on River Thames, 36m/58km W of London. During Victorian times Reading was an important manufacturing town, particularly for biscuit-making and brewing. University. Remains of Norman abbey, founded by Henry I who lies buried there.

Reading *Read.* Population: 213,474.

WEB-SITE www.reading.gov.uk

LOCAL RADIO
BBC RADIO BERKSHIRE 104.4 FM
CLASSIC GOLD 1431 AM, 2-TEN FM 97 FM

SHEFFIELD   South Yorkshire   STD Code 0114

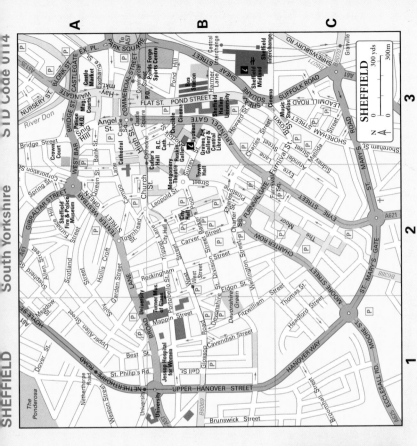

INDEX TO STREET NAMES

Allen Street	A2	Eyre Street	C2	Portobello Street	B1
Angel Street	A3	Fitzwilliam Street	B1	Queen Street	A2
Arundel Gate	B3	Flat Street	A3	Rockingham Street	B2
Arundel Street	C2	Furnace Hill	A2	St. Mary's Gate	C2
Bank Street	A3	Furnival Gate	B2	St. Mary's Road	C2
Barker's Pool	B2	Furnival Square	B2	St. Philip's Road	A1
Best Street	A1	Furnival Street	B2	Scotland Street	A2
Blonk Street	A3	Garden Street	A2	Sheaf Square	B3
Bridge Street	A3	Geil Street	A1	Sheaf Street	B3
Broad Lane	B1	Gibraltar Street	A2	Shepherd Street	A2
Broomhall Street	C1	Glossop Road	C1	Shoreham Street	C3
Brown Street	C3	Hanover Way	C1	Shrewsbury Road	C3
Brunswick Street	C1	Harmer Lane	B3	Sidney Street	C2
Campo Lane	A2	Haymarket	A3	Snig Hill	A3
Carver Street	B2	Headford Street	C1	Solly Street	A1
Castle Square	A3	High Street	A3	Spring Street	A2
Castlegate	A3	Hollis Croft	A2	Suffolk Road	C3
Cavendish Street	B1	Howard Street	B3	Surrey Street	B2
Charles Street	B2/B3	Hoyle Street	A1	Tenter Street	A2
Charter Row	C2	Leadmill Road	C3	The Moor	C2
Charter Square	B2	Leopold Street	B2	Thomas Street	C1
Church Street	A2	Mappin Street	B1	Townhead Street	A2
Commercial Street	A3	Matilda Street	C2	Trippet Lane	B2
Corporation Street	A2	Meadow Street	A1	Upper Allen Street	A1
Devonshire Street	B1	Moore Street	C2	Upper Hanover Street	B1
Division Street	B2	Netherthorpe Road	A1	Waingate	A3
Dover Street	A1	Norfolk Street	B2	Wellington Street	B2
Ecclesall Road	C1	Nursery Street	A3	West Bar	A2
Eldon Street	B2	Pinstone Street	B2	West Street	B2
Exchange Street	A3	Pond Hill	A3	Westbar Green	B3
Eyre Lane	C2	Pond Street	B3	Weston Street	A1

TOURIST INFORMATION ☎ 0114 221 1900
1 TUDOR SQUARE, SHEFFIELD, S1 2LA

HOSPITAL A & E ☎ 0114 243 4343
NORTHERN GENERAL HOSPITAL, HERRIES ROAD, SHEFFIELD, S5 7AU

COUNCIL OFFICE ☎ 0114 272 6444
FIRST POINT, 1 UNION STREET, SHEFFIELD, S1 2LA

WEB-SITE   www.sheffield.gov.uk

LOCAL RADIO   BBC RADIO SHEFFIELD 88.6 FM
MAGIC AM, SOUTH YORKSHIRE 1548 AM, HALLAM FM 97.4 FM

Sheffield S.Yorks. Population: 431,607. City, on River Don, 144m/232km NW of London. Former centre of heavy steel industry, now largely precision steel and cutlery industries. University of Sheffield and Sheffield Hallam University. Various museums dedicated to Sheffield's industrial past. National Centre for Popular Music in city centre. Meadowhall shopping centre and Sheffield City Airport, 3m/5km NE of city centre.

SOUTHAMPTON

STD Code 023

SOUTHAMPTON

0   400yds
0   400m

The Itchen Bridge (Toll)

INDEX TO STREET NAMES

Above Bar Street	B2	East Park Terrace	A2	Oxford Street	C2
Albert Road North	C3	East Street	B2	Palmerston Road	B2
Bedford Place	A1	Harbour Parade	B1	Platform Road	C2
Belvidere Road	B3	Herbert Walker	B1	Portland Terrace	B1
Bernard Street	C2	Avenue		Princes Street	A3
Brintons Road	A2	High Street	B2	Queen's Way	C2
Britannia Road	A3	Hill Lane	A1	Radcliffe Road	A3
Briton Street	C2	Howard Road	A1	St. Andrews Road	A2
Canute Road	C2	Kingsway	B2	St. Mary's Road	A2
Castle Way	B2	Landguard Road	A1	St. Mary Street	B2
Central Bridge	C2	London Road	B2	Shirley Road	A1
Central Road	C2	Marine Parade	C2	Solent Road	B1
Chapel Road	B2	Marsh Lane	B3	Southern Road	C2
Civic Centre Road	B1	Millbank Street	A3	Terminus Terrace	C2
Clovelly Road	A2	Morris Road	A1	Town Quay	C1
Commercial Road	A1	Mount Pleasant	A2	Trafalgar Road	C2
Cranbury Avenue	A2	Road		West Quay Road	B1
Cumberland Place	A1	New Road	B2	West Road	C2
Derby Road	A3	Northam Road	A3	Western	B1
Devonshire Road	A1	Ocean Way	C2	Esplanade	
Dorset Street	A2	Onslow Road	A2	Wilton Avenue	A1

TOURIST INFORMATION ☎ 023 8022 1106
9 CIVIC CENTRE ROAD,
SOUTHAMPTON, SO14 7LP

HOSPITAL A & E ☎ 023 8077 7222
SOUTHAMPTON GENERAL HOSP, TREMONA RD,
SHIRLEY, SOUTHAMPTON, SO16 6YD

COUNCIL OFFICE ☎ 023 8083 3333
CIVIC CENTRE, CIVIC CENTRE ROAD,
SOUTHAMPTON, SO14 7LY

Southampton *S'ham.* Population: 210,138. City, at confluence of Rivers Itchen and Test at head of Southampton Water, 70m/113km SW of London. Southern centre for business, culture and recreation. Container and transatlantic passenger port, dealing with 7 percent of UK's seaborne trade. Site of many famous departures: Henry V's army bound for Agincourt; the Pilgrim Fathers sailed to America on the Mayflower in 1620; maiden voyage of Queen Mary and only voyage of Titanic. Remains of medieval town walls. Medieval Merchant's House (English Heritage) has authentically recreated furnishings. Boat and helicopter ferries to Isle of Wight. Host to many international boating events including Southampton International Boat Show, Whitbread Round the World, and BT Global Challenge. University. Southampton International Airport 1m/2km S of Eastleigh.

WEB-SITE   www.southampton.gov.uk

LOCAL RADIO   BBC RADIO SOLENT 96.1 FM
CAPITAL GOLD 1557 AM, POWER FM 103.2 FM, SOUTH CITY 107.8 FM, WAVE 105.2 FM

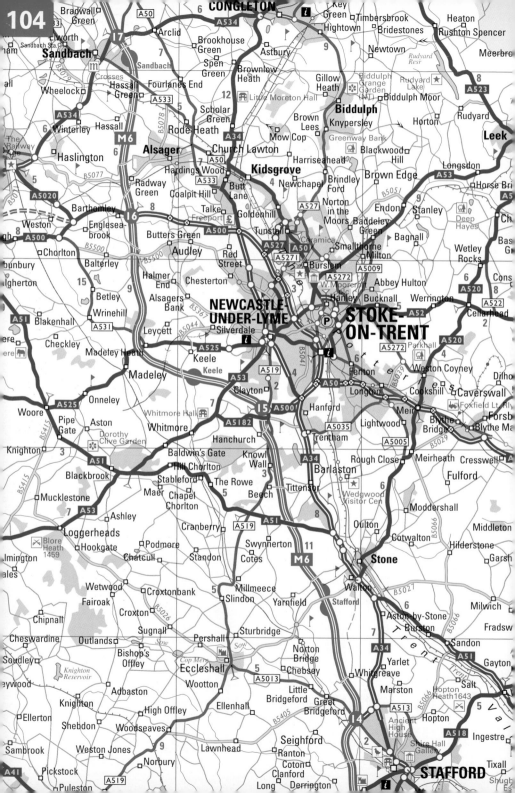

STD Code 01782

STOKE-ON-TRENT

1   **2**   **3**

HANLEY (City Centre)

Potteries Shopping Centre

Northwood Sports Centre

Waterworld
Festival Way
Festival Park
Cinema & Bowling
Marina

Bucknall Old Rd.

BUCKNALL NEW ROAD

A5010 ETRURIA ROAD

Theatre Royal
Regent Theatre

Potteries Museum & Art Gallery
Albion St.
Bus Station
Victoria Hall

Etruria Park
Mitchell Memorial Theatre
Library

Clough Street
Police Headquarters

BOTTESLOW STREET
Caldon Canal

Etruria
Etruria Industrial Museum

Fire Station

Crown & County Court

The Parkway

SHELTON NEW ROAD
Wellesley Street

Hanley

Stoke on Trent College

Hanley Cemetery

Hanley Park

QUEENSWAY
North Street

HARTSHILL ROAD

Staffordshire University

STOKE
Stoke

Staffordshire University

North Staffordshire Royal Infirmary

Fenton Manor Sports Complex

Spode Pottery
Civic Centre

River Trent

P.O. STREET
Library

A   **B**   **C**

WEB-SITE   www.stoke.gov.uk

LOCAL RADIO   BBC RADIO STOKE 94.6 FM   SIGNAL'S BIG AM 1170 AM, SIGNAL 1 102.6 FM

STOKE-ON-TRENT

N   0   500 yds

0   500m

INDEX TO STREET NAMES

Albion Street	A2	Church Street	C2	Hanley	A2	Potteries Way	A2	Stoke	C2
Ashford Street	B2	Clough Street	A1	Hartshill Road	C1	Potters Way	A3	Stoke Road	C2
Avenue Road	B2	College Road	B2	Hill Street	C1	Prince's Road	C1	Stone Street	C1
Aynsley Road	B2	Commercial Road	A3	Honeywall	C1	Quarry Avenue	C1	Stuart Road	B3
Bedford Road	B2	Copeland Street	C2	Howard Place	B2	Quarry Road	C1	Sun Street	A2
Bedford Street	B1	Dewsbury Road	C3	Ivy House Road	A3	Queen's Road	C1	The Parkway	B2
Belmont Road	A1	Eagle Street	A3	Leek Road	C2	Queensway	B1	Victoria Road	B3
Beresford Street	B2	Eastwood Road	A3	Lichfield Street	A3	Rectory Road	B2	Warner Street	A2
Boon Avenue	C1	Elenora Street	C2	Liverpool Road	C2	Regent Road	B2	Waterloo Street	A3
Botteslow Street	A3	Etruria Road	A1	Lytton Street	C2	Richmond Street	C1	Wellesley Street	B2
Boughey Road	C2	Etruria Vale Road	A1	Marsh Street	A2	Seaford Street	B2	Wellington Road	A3
Broad Street	A2	Etruscan Street	B1	Newlands Street	B2	Shelton New Road	B1	West Avenue	C1
Bucknall New Road	A3	Festival Way	A1	North Street	B1	Shelton Old Road	C1	Westland Street	C1
Bucknall Old Road	A3	Forge Lane	A1	Old Hall Street	A2	Snow Hill	B2	Yoxall Avenue	C1
Cauldon Road	B2	Glebe Street	C2	Oxford Street	C1	Stafford Street	A2		
Cemetery Road	B1	Greatbatch Avenue	C1	Parliament Row	A2	Station Road	C2		

TOURIST INFORMATION ☎ 01782 236000
POTTERIES SHOPPING CENTRE, QUADRANT RD,
STOKE-ON-TRENT, ST1 1RZ

HOSPITAL A & E ☎ 01782 715444
NORTH STAFFORDSHIRE ROYAL INFIRMARY,
PRINCE'S ROAD, STOKE-ON-TRENT, ST4 7LN

COUNCIL OFFICE ☎ 01782 234567
TOWN HALL, CIVIC CENTRE, GLEBE STREET,
STOKE-ON-TRENT, ST4 1RN

Stoke-on-Trent *Stoke* Population: 266,543. City, on River Trent, 135m/217km NW of London. Centre for employment, shopping and leisure. Created by an amalgamation of former Stoke-upon-Trent and the towns of Burslem, Fenton, Hanley, Longton and Tunstall in 1910. Capital of The Potteries (largest claywear producer in the world), now largely a finishing centre for imported pottery. Many pottery factories open to public including Wedgewood, Royal Doulton and Spode. Potteries Museum in Hanley charts history of the potteries. Gladstone Pottery Museum in Longton is centred around large bottle-kiln and demonstrates traditional skills of pottery production. Staffordshire University.

STRATFORD-UPON-AVON Warwickshire STD Code 01789

Map legend / labels visible:

A B C
3 2 1

STRATFORD-UPON-AVON
N
0 500 yds
0 500m

Picnic Area
Coach Park
Stratford Leisure, Visitor Centre & Gallery
Swannery
Marina
Butterfly & Jungle Safari
Old Tramway Walk
Cricket Ground
Stratford-upon-Avon Sports Club
Recreation Ground
Bowling and Putting Centre
Bancroft Gardens
Gower Memorial
Royal Shakespeare Theatre
Swan Theatre
Shakespeare Garden
RSC Theatre Collection
Foot Ferry
Brass Rubbing Centre
Holy Trinity
Avonbank Gardens
Mill Lane
Mill Lane
The Shakespeare Centre
Shakespeare's Birthplace
Library
Cinema
Coach Terminal
Teddy Bear Museum
American Fountain
Harvard House
Nash's House New Place Museum & Gardens
Guild Chapel
Hall's Croft
The Other Place Theatre
King Edward VI School (visitable)
Shakespeare Institute
Almshouses
Guild Chapel
Mason's Court
District Council Offices
Shakespeare Institute
Civic Hall
Town Hall
Council Offices
Police Station
Hospital
Cattle Market
Stratford-upon-Avon
Stratford-upon-Avon College
St. Andrew's Crescent
Cox's Yard
Boat Club
Lock
Stratford-upon-Avon Canal Lock

Roads: WARWICK ROAD, Welcombe Road, Maidenhead Road, Kendall Avenue, Clopton Road, BIRMINGHAM ROAD, ARDEN STREET, Western Road, Station Road, ALCESTER ROAD, Albany Road, EVESHAM ROAD, SEVEN MEADOW ROAD, A3400 SHIPSTON ROAD, BANBURY ROAD, BRIDGEWAY, CLOPTON BRIDGE, BRIDGE STREET, GUILD STREET, WOOD STREET, GROVE, Bridgetown Road, Sanctus Road, Shottery Road, Sandfield Road, Orchard Way, EVESHAM PLACE, River Avon, Avonside

INDEX TO STREET NAMES

Albany Road	B1	Great William Street	A2	Sanctus Street	C1
Alcester Road	A1	Greenhill Street	B1	Sandfield Road	C1
Arden Street	A1	Grove Road	B1	Scholar's Lane	B1
Avonside	C2	Guild Street	A2	Shakespeare Street	A2
Banbury Road	B3	Henley Street	A2	Sheep Street	B2
Bancroft Place	B3	High Street	B2	Shipston Road	C3
Birmingham Road	A1	John Street	A2	Shottery Road	B1
Bridgefoot	B3	Kendall Avenue	A2	Seven Meadow Road	C1
Bridge Street	B2	Maidenhead Road	A2	Southern Lane	C2
Bridgeway	B3	Mansell Street	A1	Station Lane	A1
Bridgetown Road	C3	Meer Street	B2	Swans Nest Lane	B3
Broad Street	C1	Mill Lane	C1	Tiddington Road	C2
Broad Walk	C1	Mulberry Street	A2	Trinity Street	C2
Bull Street	C1	Narrow Lane	C1	Tyler Street	A2
Chapel Lane	B2	New Street	C2	Union Street	B2
Chapel Street	B2	Old Town	C2	Warwick Road	A3
Cherry Orchard	C1	Old Tramway Walk	C3	Waterside	B2
Chestnut Walk	B1	Orchard Way	C1	Welcombe Road	A3
Church Street	B2	Payton Street	A2	Westbourne Grove	B1
Clopton Bridge	B3	Rother Street	B1	Western Road	A1
Clopton Road	A2	Ryland Street	C2	West Street	C1
College Lane	C2	St. Andrews	B1	Windsor Street	B2
College Street	C2	Crescent		Wood Street	B2
Ely Street	B2	St. Gregory's Road	A2		
Evesham Place	C1	Sanctus Road	C1		
Evesham Road	C1				

TOURIST INFORMATION ☎ 01789 293127
BRIDGEFOOT, STRATFORD-UPON-AVON,
WARWICKSHIRE, CV37 6GW

HOSPITAL A & E ☎ 01926 495321
WARWICK HOSPITAL, WAKIN ROAD,
WARWICK, CV34 5BW

COUNCIL OFFICE ☎ 01789 267575
COUNCIL OFFICES, ELIZABETH HOUSE,
CHURCH ST, STRATFORD-UPON-AVON, CV37 6HX

Stratford-upon-Avon (Also called Stratford-on-Avon.) *Works*. Population: 22,231. Town, on River Avon, 8m/13km SW of Warwick. Tourist centre. Many attractive 16c buildings. Reconstructed Shakespeare's Birthplace. Elizabethan garden at New Place. Hall's Croft Elizabethan town house and doctor's dispensary. Royal Shakespeare Theatre. Shakespeare's grave at Holy Trinity Church. Anne Hathaway's Cottage to W, at Shottery.

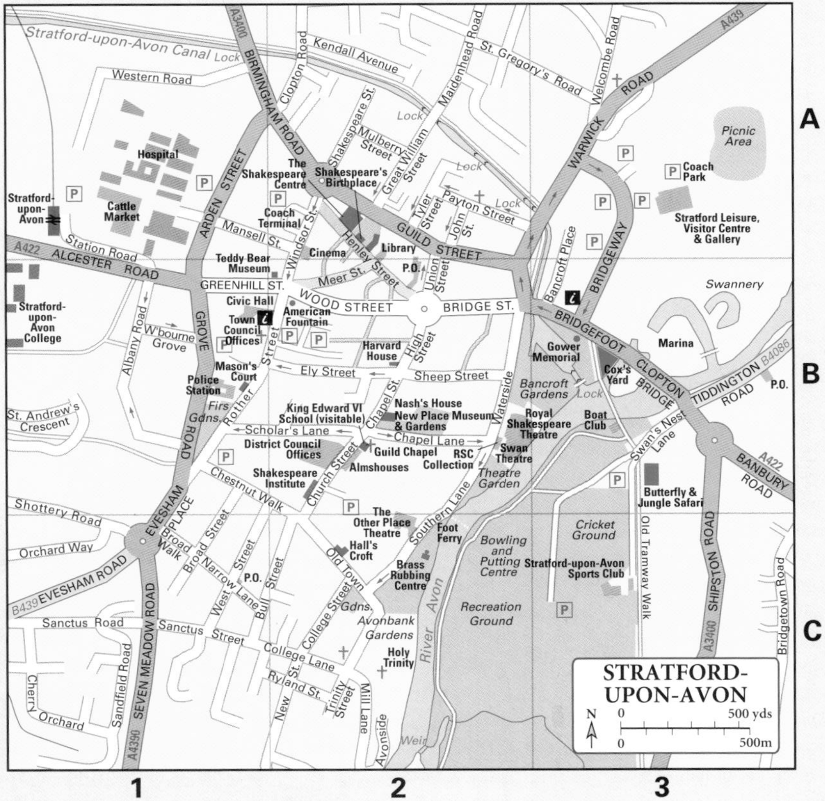

WEB-SITE www.stratford.gov.uk

LOCAL RADIO BBC RADIO COVENTRY & WARWICKSHIRE 94.8 & 103.7 FM
102 FM - THE BEAR 102 FM

SOUTH SHIELDS
NORTH SHIELDS
SUNDERLAND
SEAHAM
Easington Colliery
Turning the Tide
Horden
Easington
Little Thorpe
Cold Hesledon
Nose's Point
Dalton-le-Dale
Seaton
Hawthorn
Murton
South Hetton
Haswell
Shotton
Sherburn
Carrville
Pittington
Littletown
Sherburn
Ludworth
DURHAM
Cathedral
Neville's Cross
Bearpark
Ushaw Moor
Esh Winning
Esh
Quebec
Langley Park
Sacriston
Witton Gilbert
Kimblesworth
Edmondsley
Waldridge
Waldridge Fell
CHESTER-LE-STREET
Pelton
Newfield
Ouston
Beamish
Beamish Open Air Museum
Grange Villa
South Moor
STANLEY
Annfield Plain
CONSETT
Delves
Leadgate
Iveston
Medomsley
Dipton
Hamsterley
Ebchester
Chopwell
High Spen
Rowlands Gill
Highfield
Lintzford
Blackhall Mill
Hamsterley
Burnopfield
Tantobie
Tanfield
Marley Hill
Sunniside
WHICKHAM
Swalwell
Winlaton
Blaydon
Stella
Ryton
Crawcrook
Wylam
Prudhoe
Coalburns
Greenside
Barlow
NEWCASTLE UPON TYNE
GATESHEAD
FELLING
Heworth
Pelaw
Bill Quay
Walker
Byker
Heaton
Jesmond
Gosforth
Longbenton
Wallsend
Willington
Denton Burn
Blakelaw
Fenham
Newburn
Lemington
Throckley
Heddon-on-the-Wall
Callerton Lane End
Rudchester
Whitley Bay
Whitburn
Marsden
Cleadon
East Boldon
West Boldon
BOLDON
Hebburn
Jarrow
Monkton
Wardley
Hetton-le-Hole
HOUGHTON-LE-SPRING
Newbottle
Penshaw
Herrington
Shiney Row
Philadelphia
Fatfield
WASHINGTON
Birtley
Angel of the North
Lamesley
Kibblesworth
Team Valley
Springwell
Wrekenton
Low Fell
Ouston
Pelton Fell
Great Lumley
Little Lumley
Bournmoor
Fence Houses
Colliery Row
West Rainton
East Rainton
Framwellgate Moor
Pity Me
Plawsworth
Chester Moor
Craghead
Holmside
Burnhope
Maiden Law
Lanchester
Langley Park
Cornsay Colliery
Satley
Butsfield
Roker
Fulwell
Southwick
Monkwearmouth
National Glass Centre
Hendon
Ryhope
New Silksworth
Silksworth
South Hylton
Hylton
Castletown
New Silksworth
Hastings Hill
Tursdale

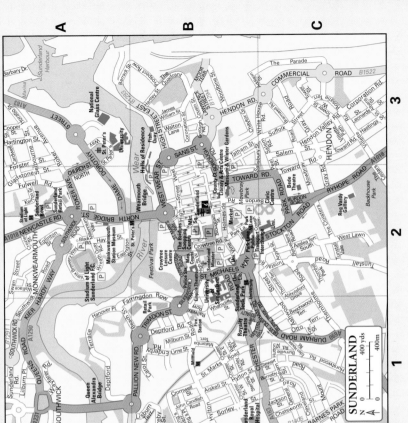

SUNDERLAND

Tyne & Wear

STD Code 0191

TOURIST INFORMATION ☎ 0191 553 2000
50 FAWCETT STREET, SUNDERLAND, SR1 1RF

HOSPITAL A & E ☎ 0191 565 6256
SUNDERLAND DISTRICT GENERAL HOSPITAL,
KAYLL ROAD, SUNDERLAND, SR4 7TP

COUNCIL OFFICE ☎ 0191 553 1000
SUNDERLAND CITY COUNCIL, CIVIC CENTRE, BURDON
ROAD, SUNDERLAND, SR2 7DN

Sunderland *T. & W.* Population 183,310. Industrial city and seaport at mouth of River Wear, 11m/17km SE of Newcastle upon Tyne. Previously largest ship-building town in the world: coal mining was also important. Several museums celebrate city's industrial past. Service sector and manufacturing account for largest contribution to local economy. National Glass Centre commemorates importance of stained glass to area. University. Airport 4m/6km W.

WEB-SITE www.sunderland.gov.uk

LOCAL RADIO
BBC RADIO NEWCASTLE 95.4 FM, 1458 AM
SUN FM 103.4 FM

SWANSEA

STD Code 01792

INDEX TO STREET NAMES

Albert Row	C2	Gors Avenue	A1	Page Street	B2
Alexandra Road	B2	Grove Place	B2	Pentre Guinea	A3
Argyle Street	C1	Gwent Road	A1	Road	
Beach Street	C1	Hanover Street	B1	Pen-y-Craig Road	A1
Belle Vue Way	B2	High Street	B2	Powys Avenue	A1
Bond Street	C1	Islwyn Road	A1	Princess Way	B2
Brooklands Terrace	B1	King Edward's	C1	Rose Hill	B1
Brynmor	C1	Road		St. Helen's Avenue	C1
Crescent		Llangyfelach Road	A2	St. Helen's Road	C1
Brynymor Road	C1	Lower Oxford	C1	St. Mary Street	B2
Burrows Place	C3	Street		Singleton Street	C2
Cambrian Place	C3	Mackworth Street	B3	Somerset Place	C3
Carmarthen Road	A2	Mansel Street	B1	South Guildhall	C1
Castle Street	B2	Mayhill Road	A1	Road	
Clarence Terrace	C2	Morris Lane	B3	Strand	B3
Constitution Hill	B1	Mount Pleasant	B2	Terrace Road	B2
Cromwell Street	B1	Mumbles Road	C1	The Kingsway	B2
De La Beche Street	B2	Neath Road	A3	Townhill Road	A1
Delhi Street	B3	New Cut Road	B3	Vincent Street	C1
Dyfatty Street	B2	New Orchard	A2	Walter Road	C1
Dyfed Avenue	B1	Street		Waun-Wen Road	A2
East Burrows Road	C3	North Hill Road	A2	Wellington Street	C2
Fabian Way	B3	Orchard Street	B2	Westbury Street	C1
Foxhole Road	A3	Oystermouth	C1	Western Street	C1
Glamorgan Street	C2	Road		West Way	C2

TOURIST INFORMATION ☎ 01792 468321
WESTWAY,
SWANSEA, SA1 3QG

HOSPITAL A & E ☎ 01792 702222
MORRISTON HOSPITAL, MORRISTON,
SWANSEA, SA6 6NL

COUNCIL OFFICE ☎ 01792 636000
COUNTY HALL, OYSTERMOUTH ROAD,
SWANSEA, SA1 3SN

WEB-SITE www.swansea.gov.uk

LOCAL RADIO BBC RADIO WALES 93.9 FM
SWANSEA SOUND 1170 AM

Swansea (Abertawe). Population: 171,038. City, port on Swansea Bay at mouth of River Tawe, and Wales' second city, 35m/57km W of Cardiff. Settlement developed next to Norman castle built in 1099, but claims made that a Viking settlement existed before this date. Previously a port for local metal smelting industries. Bombed in World War II, and city centre rebuilt. Birthplace of Dylan Thomas, who described it as 'an ugly, lovely town'. Remains of 14c castle (Cadw) or fortified manor house. University of Wales. Tropical plant and wildlife leisure centre, Plantasia. Airport 5m/9km W at Fairwood Common.

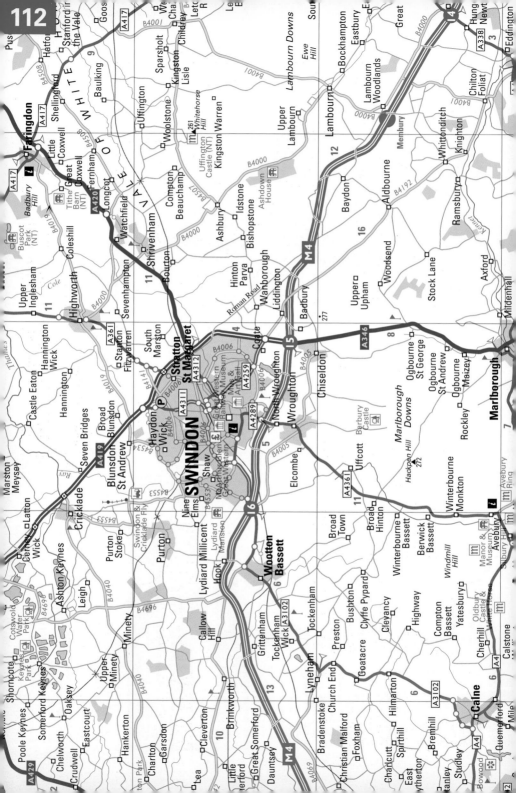

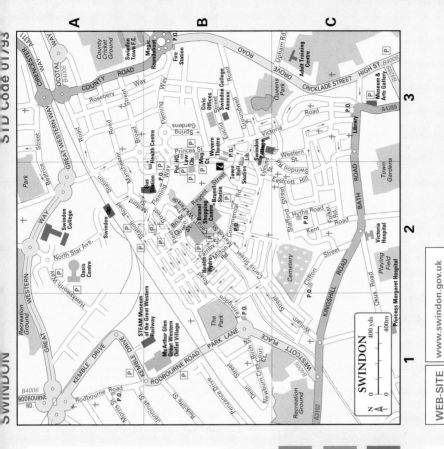

SWINDON

STD Code 01793

WEB-SITE www.swindon.gov.uk

LOCAL RADIO BBC WILTSHIRE SOUND 103.6 FM
CLASSIC GOLD 1161 AM, GWR FM 972 FM

INDEX TO STREET NAMES

TOURIST INFORMATION ☎ 01793 530328
37 REGENT STREET,
SWINDON, SN1 1JL

HOSPITAL A & E ☎ 01793 536231
PRINCESS MARGARET HOSPITAL, OKUS ROAD,
SWINDON, SN1 4JU

COUNCIL OFFICE ☎ 01793 463000
CIVIC OFFICES, EUCLID STREET,
SWINDON, SN1 2JH

Swindon *Swin.* Population: 145,236. Town, industrial and commercial centre, 70m/113km W of London. Large, modern shopping centre. Town expanded considerably in 19c with arrival of the railway. The Museum of the Great Western Railway exhibits Swindon built locomotives and documents the history of the railway works.

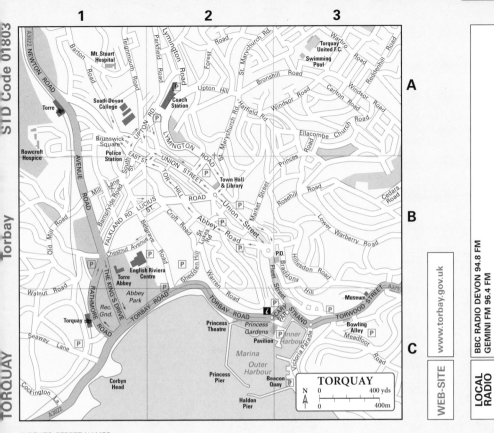

STD Code 01803

Torbay

TORQUAY

WEB-SITE www.torbay.gov.uk

LOCAL RADIO BBC RADIO DEVON 94.8 FM GEMINI FM 96.4 FM

TORQUAY
N 0   400 yds
0   400m

INDEX TO STREET NAMES

TOURIST INFORMATION ☎ 01803 297428
VAUGHAN PARADE,
TORQUAY, TQ2 5JG

HOSPITAL A & E ☎ 01803 614567
TORBAY HOSPITAL, NEWTON ROAD,
TORQUAY, TQ2 7AA

COUNCIL OFFICE ☎ 01803 201201
TOWN HALL, CASTLE CIRCUS,
TORQUAY, TQ1 3DR

Torquay *Torbay* Population: 59,587. Town, 18m/30km S of Exeter. Chief town and resort of Torbay English Riviera district, with harbour and several beaches. Noted for mild climate. Torre Abbey with 15c gatehouse, is a converted monastery housing a collecion of furniture and glassware. Torquay Museum has display on crimewriter Agatha Christie born in Torquay. Kent's Cavern showcaves are an important prehistoric site. Babbacombe Model village 2m/3km N.

STD Code 01962

Hampshire

WINCHESTER

WINCHESTER

N 0   500 yds

0   500m

BBC RADIO SOLENT 96.1 FM
OCEAN FM 96.7 FM, WIN 107.2 FM

LOCAL RADIO

www.winchester.gov.uk

WEB-SITE

INDEX TO STREET NAMES

**TOURIST INFORMATION ☎ 01962 840500
GUILDHALL, THE BROADWAY, WINCHESTER
HAMPSHIRE, SO23 9LJ**

**HOSPITAL A & E ☎ 01962 863535
ROYAL HAMPSHIRE COUNTY HOSPITAL,
ROMSEY ROAD, WINCHESTER, SO22 5DG**

**COUNCIL OFFICE ☎ 01962 840222
CITY OFFICES, COLEBROOK STREET,
WINCHESTER, SO23 9LJ**

Winchester *Hants.* Population: 36,121. City, county town on River Itchen on site of Roman town of Venta Belgarum, 12m/19km N of Southampton. Ancient capital of Wessex and of Anglo-Saxon England. 11c cathedral, longest in Europe with carved Norman font and England's oldest complete choir-stalls. Winchester College, boys' public school founded 1382. 13c Great Hall is only remaining part of Winchester Castle. Westgate Museum is in 12c gatehouse in medieval city wall, once a debtors' prison. 12c hospital of St. Cross. City Mill (National Trust), built over river in 18c. To S across river, St. Catherine's Hill, Iron Age fort. Extensive ruins of medieval Wolvesey Castle, also known as Old Bishop's Palace (English Heritage), 1m/2km SE.

WINDSOR Windsor & Maidenhead STD Code 01753

WINDSOR

0 ___ 400 yds
0 ___ 400m

WEB-SITE www.rbwm.gov.uk

LOCAL RADIO BBC RADIO BERKSHIRE 95.4 FM
STAR FM 106.6 FM

INDEX TO STREET NAMES

Alexandra Road	C1
Alma Road	A3
Arthur Road	B2
Barry Avenue	A2
Bolton Avenue	C2
Bolton Road	C2
Bulkeley Avenue	B1
Charles Street	B2
Clarence Road	C2
Datchet Road	B3
Eton & Windsor Relief Road	A3
Frances Road	B1
Goslar Way	A1
Green Lane	C2
Grove Road	B1
High Street (Eton)	A3
High Street (Windsor)	B3

Imperial Road	C2
King Edward VII Avenue	B2
Kings Road	B2
Meadow Lane	A2
Osborne Road	C2
Oxford Road	C2
Parsonage Lane	B1
Peascod Street	B2
St. Leonards Road	C2
Sheet Street	B3
Springfield Road	C1
Stovell Road	A1
Thames Street	A3
The Long Walk	C3
Vansittart Road	B2
Victoria Street	B2
York Avenue	C1

TOURIST INFORMATION ☎ 01753 743900
24 HIGH STREET,
WINDSOR, SL4 1LH

HOSPITAL A & E ☎ 01753 633000
WEXHAM PARK HOSPITAL, WEXHAM STREET,
SLOUGH, SL2 4HL

COUNCIL OFFICE ☎ 01753 810525
COUNCIL OFFICES, YORK HOUSE, SHEET STREET,
WINDSOR, SL4 1DD

Windsor *W. & M.* Population: 26,369. Town, attractive market town on S bank of River Thames, 2m/3km S of Slough and 21m/34km W of London. Castle is royal residence. Great Park to S of town is open to public; Home Park bordering river is private. St. George's Chapel is impressive. Many Georgian houses, and guildhall designed by Sir Christopher Wren.

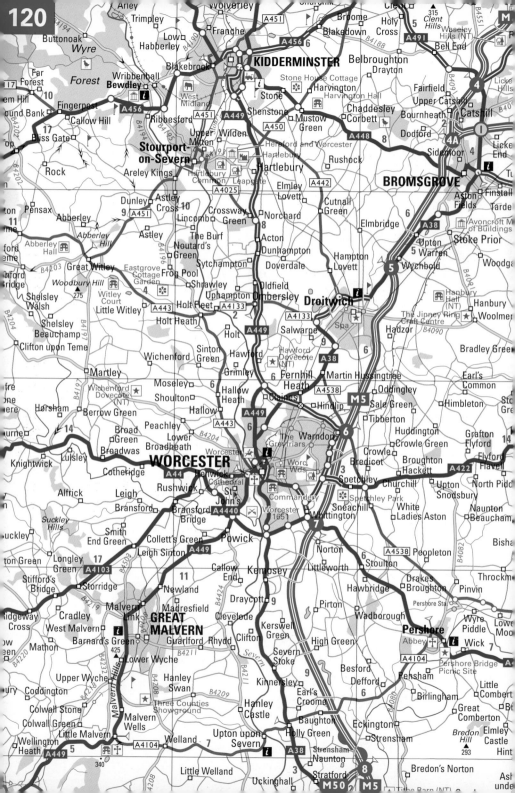

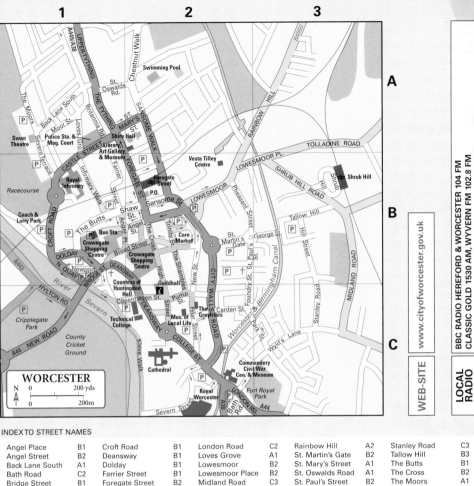

Worcestershire · STD Code 01905 · **WORCESTER**

INDEX TO STREET NAMES

TOURIST INFORMATION ☎ 01905 726311
THE GUILDHALL, HIGH STREET,
WORCESTER, WR1 2EY

HOSPITAL A & E ☎ 01905 763333
WORCESTER ROYAL INFIRMARY, RONKSWOOD
HOSPITAL, NEWTOWN ROAD, WR5 1HN

COUNCIL OFFICE ☎ 01905 723471
THE GUILDHALL, HIGH STREET,
WORCESTER, WR1 2EY

Worcester *Worcs.* Population: 82,661. City, on River Severn, 24m/38km SW of Birmingham. Shopping, cultural, sports and industrial centre; industries include porcelain and sauces and condiments. 18c guildhall. Cathedral mainly Early English includes England's largest Norman crypt, 13c choir and Lady Chapel and tomb of King John. Three Choirs Festival held here every third year. Civil War Centre at the Commandery, headquarters for Charles II during Battle of Worcester. Factory tours and museum at Royal Worcester Porcelain. Elgar's Birthplace, home of composer Sir Edward Elgar, in Broadheath, 3m/5km W.

A64

Bulmer

Welburn

Stillington
Farlington
Sheriff Hutton
Whitwell-on-the-Hill
Kirkham

Alne
Cross Lanes
23
Huby
West Lilling
Thornton-le-Clay
Foston
Crambe

Tollerton
Youlton
Sutton-on-the-Forest
Sutton Park
Barton-le-Willo

Idwark

Linton-on-Ouse
Newton-on-Ouse
A19
Strensall
Flaxton
Harton
Howsl

Nun Monkton
Beningbrough Hall (NT)
Shipton
Strensall Common
Sand Hutton
Scrayingham
Lepp
Bossall

Beningbrough
Wigginton
Towthorpe
18
Claxton
Buttercrambe

Moor Monkton
Haxby
Earswick
Upper Helmsley
A64

Skelton
A1237
Huntington
Stockton on the Forest
Warthill
Stamford Bridge

A59
15
Roman Road
Overton
New Earswick
Brockfield
Holtby
A166
Gate Helmsley
Stamford Bridge 1066
Full Sutto

Marston Moor
Nether Poppleton
Rawcliffe
A19
A1036
Minster
Murton
Low Catton
High Catton

kwith
Marston Moor 1644
Hessay
Upper Poppleton
YORK
Osbaldwick
Dunnington

Long Marston
Knapton
Nat Ry Museum
Jorvik
11
Wilber

B1224
Rufforth
Acomb
A1237
A1036
Clifford's Tower
Heslington
A1079
Kexby

Bilton
Hutton Wandesley
i
Fulford
B1228
Newton upon Derwen

Angram
Askham Bryan
York
A64
Elvington

Healaugh
Askham Richard
10
Bishopthorpe
McArthurGlen
Crockey Hill
Sutton upon Derwent

Wighill
Bilbrough
Copmanthorpe
Naburn
14
Deighton
Wheldrake
Storwood

Catterton
Acaster Malbis
Colton
Escrick
Thicket Priory
East Cottingwith
Ross Moor

wton Kyme
A64
Thor

Tadcaster
Acaster Selby
Thorganby
Ellerton

59
Kirkby Wharfe
Appleton Roebuck
Ouse B1122
Skipwith
Aughton
Foggathor

A162
Bolton Percy
Stillingfleet
Kelfield
North Duffield
Har

9
Ulleskelf
Wharfe B1223
Cawood
Riccall
Bubwith
Highfield

Saxton
Ryther
Wistow
A163
Gunby
Breighton

n Hall
Barkston
Church Fenton
Osgodby
South Duffield
B1228

in Elmet
Little Fenton
Biggin
B1223
Barlby
Lund

Newthorpe
Thorpe Willoughby
i
Selby
Cliffe
Wressle
Brin

Steeton Hall Gatehouse
South Milford
Hambleton
8
Brayton
A63
12
Howde St

Lumby
Monk Fryston
A63
Hemingbrough
Newsholme

3
Hillam
Gateforth
Burn
A19
Barlow
Long Drax
Barmby on the Marsh
Knedlington
Asselby

A162
West Haddlesey
A1041
7
5

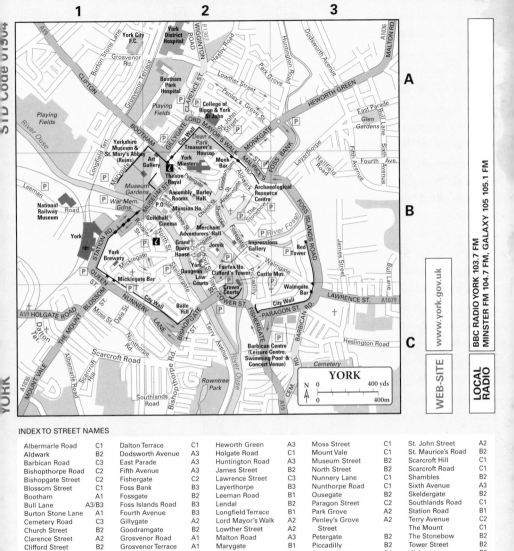

YORK

INDEX TO STREET NAMES

TOURIST INFORMATION ☎ 01904 554488
TIC TRAVEL OFFICE, 20 GEORGE HUDSON ST.,
YORK, YO1 6WR

HOSPITAL A & E ☎ 01904 631313
YORK DISTRICT HOSPITAL, WIGGINTON ROAD,
YORK, YO31 8HE

COUNCIL OFFICE ☎ 01904 613161
THE GUILDHALL,
YORK, YO1 9QN

York Population: 124,609. City, ancient city and archiepiscopal see on River Ouse, 22m/36km NE of Leeds. On site of Roman Eboracum. Constantine the Great proclaimed Roman Emperor in York in AD 306; only emperor to be enthroned in Britain. City fell to Danes in AD 867 and became known as Jorvik. Medieval wall largely intact, other fortifications including Clifford's Tower (English Heritage). York Minster has largest Medieval stained glass window in country. Previously a wool trading, craft and railway centre. Home to National Railway Museum. Jorvik Viking Centre in Coppergate. Merchant Adventurers' Hall in Fossgate is finest remaining guildhall in Europe. University of York at Heslington. Racecourse at Knavesmire.

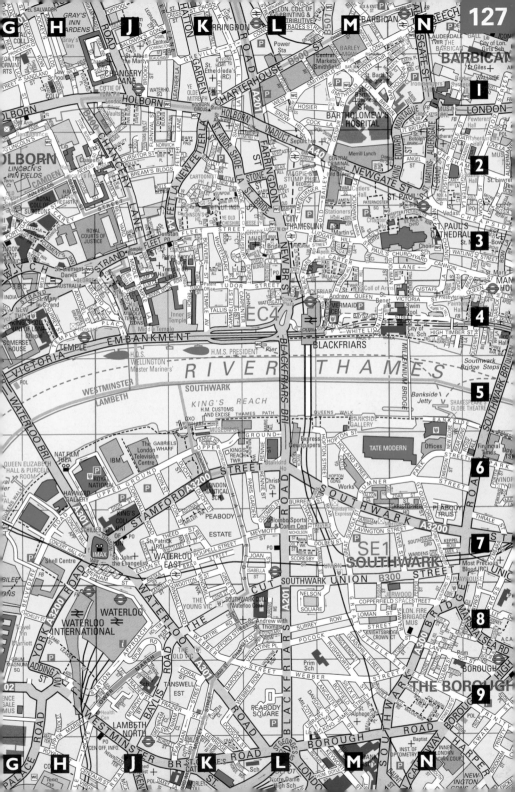

INDEX TO LONDON STREET NAMES

General Abbreviations

All	Alley	Ch	Church	Dr	Drive	Grds	Grounds	Mkt	Market	Quad	Quadrant	TH	Town Hall
Allot	Allotments	Chyd	Churchyard	Dws	Dwellings	Grn	Green	Mkts	Markets	RC	Roman Catholic	Tenn	Tennis
Amb	Ambulance	Cin	Cinema	E	East	Grns	Greens	Ms	Mews	Rd	Road	Ter	Terrace
App	Approach	Circ	Circus	Ed	Education	Gro	Grove	Mt	Mount	Rds	Roads	Thea	Theatre
Arc	Arcade	Cl/Clo	Close	Elec	Electricity	Gros	Groves	Mus	Museum	Rec	Recreation	Trd	Trading
Av/Ave	Avenue	Co	County	Embk	Embankment	Gt	Great	N	North	Res	Reservoir	Twr	Tower
Bdy	Broadway	Coll	College	Est	Estate	Ho	House	N T	National Trust	Ri	Rise	Twrs	Towers
Bk	Bank	Comm	Community	Ex	Exchange	Hos	Houses	Nat	National	S	South	Uni	University
Bldgs	Buildings	Conv	Convent	Exhib	Exhibition	Hosp	Hospital	PH	Public House	Sch	School	Vil	Villa, Villas
Boul	Boulevard	Coron	Coroners	FB	Footbridge	Hts	Heights	PO	Post Office	Sec	Secondary	View	View
Bowl	Bowling	Cors	Corners	FC	Football Club	Ind	Industrial	Par	Parade	Sh	Shop	W	West
Br/Bri	Bridge	Cotts	Cottages	Fld	Field	Int	International	Pas	Passage	Shop	Shopping	Wd	Wood
Bus	Business	Cov	Covered	Flds	Fields	Junct	Junction	Pav	Pavilion	Sq	Square	Wds	Woods
C of E	Church of England	Crem	Crematorium	Fm	Farm	La	Lane	Pk	Park	St	Saint	Wf	Wharf
Cath	Cathedral	Cres	Crescent	Gall	Gallery	Las	Lanes	Pl	Place	St	Street	Wk	Walk
Cem	Cemetery	Ct	Court	Gar	Garage	Lib	Library	Pol	Police	Sta	Station	Wks	Works
Cen	Central, Centre	Ctyd	Courtyard	Gdn	Garden	Lo	Lodge	Prec	Precinct	Sts	Streets	Yd	Yard
Cft	Croft	Cts	Courts	Gdns	Gardens	Lwr	Lower	Prim	Primary	Sub	Subway		
Cfts	Crofts	Dep	Depot	Govt	Government	Mag	Magistrates	Prom	Promenade	Swim	Swimming		
		Dev	Development	Gra	Grange	Mans	Mansions	Pt	Point	TA	Territorial Army		
				Grd	Ground	Mem	Memorial						